JAMIE KENNEDY'S
SEASONS

JAMIE KENNEDY'S
SEASONS

WHITECAP BOOKS

VANCOUVER / TORONTO / NEW YORK

The information in this book is true and complete to the best of our knowledge.
All recommendations are made without guarantee on the part of the author or
Whitecap Books Ltd. The author and publisher disclaim any liability in connection
with the use of this information. For additional information, please contact
Whitecap Books Ltd., 351 Lynn Avenue, North Vancouver, BC V7J 2C4.

Edited by Alison Maclean
Proofread by Kathy Evans
Design by Tanya Lloyd/Spotlight Designs
Color photographs by Michael Mahovlich
Food styling by Jamie Kennedy
Prop styling by Oksana Slavutych

Printed and bound in Canada.

Canadian Cataloguing in Publication Data

Kennedy, Jamie.
Jamie Kennedy's seasons

Includes index.
ISBN 1-55285-006-4

1. Cookery. I. Title. II. Title: Seasons.
TX714.K46 2000   641.5   C00-911183-2

The publisher acknowledges the support of the Canada Council and the Cultural
Services Branch of the Government of British Columbia in making this publication
possible. We acknowledge the financial support of the Government of Canada through
the Book Publishing Industry Development Program for our publishing activities.

For Lorren, Mum, Dad, Julia, Micha, Jackson, and Nile

Acknowledgements

Thanks to Robert McCullough and Whitecap Books for approaching me about this project.
Thanks to the food service and hospitality industry, which continues to enrich my life daily
with new challenges and interesting people. A special thank you to my new friend and
the editor of this book, Alison Maclean, for teaching me English and encouraging me so
much throughout the process of writing. Another special thank you to everyone at JK ROM.
Without the confidence you have instilled in me, this book would not have been possible.
Our work together makes ideas come alive.

With Lorren.

With Robert, Nicole, Mum, and Dad.

Clodagh Moss at JK ROM.

David Pell at JK ROM.

Contents

Palmerston Garden.

JK ROM staff on the terrace.

Palmerston staff during service.

With Lloyd, catering.

Foreword

I have been an admirer of Jamie Kennedy's cooking and his approach to food for more than two decades. As a chef, he's been talked about from the beginning of his career, that first public recognition coming in the early '80s at Scaramouche, the restaurant that heralded a new phase of culinary history in Toronto. He enhanced his profile with the opening of his own restaurant, Palmerston. But nowhere has he been more appreciated than in the restaurant he now owns in the Royal Ontario Museum, Jamie Kennedy at the ROM. Contemporary food, beautifully served, just steps away from Chinese treasures, dinosaurs, and West Coast totem poles. Here Kennedy cooks at the full measure of his profession, with style, grace, skill, and passion—trusting his instincts, confident through experience, and simplifying as he focuses on the intensity of flavors.

Kennedy has not been alone as his profession emerged in Canada. In the same decades he has been distilling his culinary style, there has grown up in Canada a vibrant new generation of young cooks and chefs, a culinary cohort who are proud to call their new style of cooking Canadian. Kennedy has been a leading chef of this brigade—he has had a hand in training and inspiring many younger chefs. Kennedy's food is Canadian, not because he is a proponent of the butter-tart-Nanaimo-bar Canadiana, but because he understands the fundamentals of what makes a cuisine. It's about ingredients,

in their place and in their time. Aptly titled *Jamie Kennedy's Seasons*, his new cookbook bears witness to his passion for food—passion well founded in life-long curiosity about all things edible. I like that as a kid at public school he ran home at lunchtime so he could watch Julia Child on television. "She cast a spell on me," Kennedy confesses. "I fell in love with the process and the magic." And, as a teen, Kennedy rounded up fellow foodies at high school to form a culinary club. That young age now astounds him as he is the father of a 16-year-old daughter, appropriately named Julia. *Jamie Kennedy's Seasons*, published 15 years after his first, the *Jamie Kennedy Cookbook*, demonstrates a profound knowledge of the food of Canada. And that is why "Seasons" is so appropriate as a title, for the four quarters of the year frame the way Kennedy approaches food. "Everything about food becomes more understandable when you use the seasons as your guide," Kennedy explains. "It's a really honest way of looking at cooking."

Reading through *Jamie Kennedy's Seasons* reveals the parameters these ingredients give him in the kitchen. His recipes, based on his restaurant menus, feature the foods as they grow in your garden, or appear, not so much in the supermarket, as in markets—fiddleheads, morels, asparagus for the spring, a luxury of eggplant, tomatoes, salmon, young carrots and fresh herbs mark a Canadian summer, the lusty flavors of sunchokes, squash, lentils, corn, bacon, and roasted vegetables herald cool autumnal evenings, and for winter, onions, celery root, blue cheese, smoked black cod, potatoes, blood oranges, lamb and comfy meatloaf to see a soul through the season's bleakness. It's like running your finger along a shopping list of the reality of a northern clime.

I found it refreshing to find such a proponent of preserving in this day of imported year-round-availability of almost every item of produce. An example comes up in his winter-time vegetarian Eggplant Gateau with Creamy Polenta, prepared a la Kennedy with food preserved in the summer. "Of course," he speaks to the reader/cook in the recipe lead, "if you haven't done any preserving, these vegetables are still available fresh in the winter. The problem is of course that they are super expensive," and he delivers the final coup de grace, "and taste like cardboard." Not many cookbook authors are that blunt—but that's Kennedy's philosophy, and it was the search for the finest quality produce that provoked him and friend, fellow chef Michael Stadtländer to found Forks and Knives, an alliance of organic growers and chefs. "Not", Kennedy added, "just because the ingredients are organic, but because growers of organic foods were the only ones who could provide ingredients fresher, more flavorful, at their peak." Local counts too, because food that comes from afar is bred for travelling, and picked underripe to make sure it makes it to the market intact.

On a practical note, Kennedy presents recipes in a way any interested cook who wants to take time to cook can understand and cook from. There are some quick recipes, the kind you can execute in a few minutes, an example being spring's Chive Cream Soup, a peasant-ly simple whirl of onion, potatoes, chicken stock, chives and cream, but most take the kind of preparation you expect in a chef's book and get the layering and intensity of flavors and the distinguishing professional presentation. "This is not," according to Kennedy, "an *I hate to Cook Cookbook*, nor is it the *Joy of Cooking*." Rather, *Jamie Kennedy's Seasons* reflects Kennedy's wide ranging food interests as witnessed by the dishes he has cooked for his patrons.

Kennedy is writing for young chefs too. He wants to show them how to start recipes. "There is a logic to how to go about cooking a recipe," explains Kennedy, "and I fought to have presentation tips for all the recipes. Presentation is not superfluous. It's integral to the dish, and something I think is very important. It should come out of the ingredients in the dish."

There is nothing I like better in a cookbook than to feel as if I am cooking along with an expert. I wasn't disappointed. Kennedy has the cook right beside him, with his little asides, with his clearly written methods, explaining why rather than just telling you how. He's there with the experience of one of Canada's premier chefs as you read, plot, and execute your next foray into the kitchen. *Jamie Kennedy's Seasons* is truly original, truly personal and reflects the quality of his cooking that has made me an admirer since the '80s and will keep me there.

— Elizabeth Baird, Food Editor,
Canadian Living magazine

Introduction

Fifteen years have passed since I wrote my last book. Writing *Seasons* has been a wonderful opportunity to take stock; to compare who I was then with who I have become, professionally speaking. It is interesting for me to note that many of the thoughts and ideas that were important to me then still resonate today. My approach to cooking still isn't trendy. Rather, I have adhered to classic precepts. As I've grown as a cook, I have consistently tried to distill my knowledge and to present food with clean lines and recognizable tastes.

This book is a look at some of the recipes I have developed over the last fifteen years. These are not recipes for the "I hate to cook" cook. They celebrate the art and nuance of cooking. Some take longer to prepare than others, some are more difficult than others, but they are all written from the point of view of a professional cook interpreting for the home cook.

As someone who uses food as a form of expression, I have set parameters on my thinking so a style of cooking has emerged that echoes who I am. Framing my cooking within the seasons as they relate to people living in Southern Ontario gives me a platform for my creativity. The notion of preserving fruits and vegetables in the summer and fall and using them in winter and spring recipes helps to focus my creative energy and is an honest response to where I live. Good results are more easily attained when we focus on the produce that's available locally and seasonally.

You will find several cross-references in this book between fresh ingredients of one season being preserved for use in another. This is not a new approach to cooking; it's how people fed their families before the advent of "global shopping" in which there is no such thing as seasons. Cooking with seasonal produce has new significance today because it's now about supporting the local economy. It is also a recognition of the artisanal approach to growing produce and processing food, and it flies nicely in the face of agri-business and poor stewardship of the land.

Seasons is foremost a celebration of seasonal cooking, but it also celebrates differences in cuisines. Since I'm not tradition-bound in my approach to cooking, living in an urban center

Staff meal at Scaramouche.

with a huge ethnic variety has been a great opportunity to observe and incorporate several new global influences. I also enjoy the chance to explore the exotic ingredients in the various food markets in Toronto. One can literally shop the world without leaving the city. These influences, along with seasonal ones, have allowed new notes to emerge in my cooking style. The development of that style—as with any cook's—is a slow and continuing process.

I hope that I succeed in communicating the spirit with which this book was written—that it is really your approach to cooking that matters the most. We need to trust our sense of taste and our cooking techniques so we can free up the right hand that once held the recipe book and the left hand that once held the measuring spoons. Then we can create with our whole imaginations.

Jamie at Palmerston relaxing after service.

Ken, Thaya, and Monique at Superior.

Basics

Jamie catering in 1983.

Chicken Stock

4 lb./2 kg chicken bones
6 cups/1.5 litres cold water

FOR THE BOUQUET GARNI:
2 onions, split crosswise
2 carrots, washed and split lengthwise
2 stalks celery, washed and split lengthwise

1 leek, washed and split lengthwise
10 black peppercorns, crushed
2 bay leaves
2 whole cloves
2 sprigs fresh thyme
    or
$^1/_2$ tsp./2 mL dried thyme

▶ Yields 6 cups/1.5 litres

Place the bones and water in a stock pot and bring to a boil. Reduce to a simmer and skim surface to remove any scum.

Add bouquet garni and simmer, uncovered, 3 to 4 hours. Strain liquid through cheesecloth and discard everything else.

Use as required or freeze for later use.

Tomato Consommé

4 lb./2 kg very ripe tomatoes
3 cloves garlic
1 leek, well washed
1 small celery heart or 2 stalks

12 leaves fresh basil or 1 Tbsp./15 mL dried
1 tsp./5 mL freshly grated nutmeg
4 egg whites
Salt to taste
10 grinds freshly ground black pepper

▶ Yields 6 cups/1.5 litres

Coarsely chop tomatoes, garlic, leek, celery, and basil. Process vegetables approximately 5 seconds in food processor or dice in small pieces. Transfer to a large, heavy-bottomed soup pot. Add nutmeg, egg whites, salt and pepper, and bring quickly to a boil. When raft forms, reduce heat and simmer 2 hours. Strain consommé through cheesecloth. Use as required or freeze for later use.

Beef, Lamb, or Chicken Jus

3 lbs./1.5 kg beef, lamb, or chicken bones, cut into
    1- to 2-inch/2.5- to 5-cm pieces

Mirepoix of 2 onions, 1 carrot, 1 stalk celery

5 cloves garlic, roughly chopped

$1/2$ small tin tomato paste

15 dried juniper berries, crushed

1 sprig fresh thyme
    or
$1/2$ tsp./2 mL dried thyme

3 bay leaves

1 sprig fresh rosemary
    or
$1/2$ tsp./2 mL dried rosemary

12 black peppercorns, crushed

$1 1/4$ cups/300 mL red wine

▶ Yields 4 cups/950 mL

Preheat an oven to 400°F/200°F.

    Spread bones in a roasting pan and roast until browned, about 1 hour. Add mirepoix and garlic and continue browning in oven another 30 minutes. Add tomato paste and continue browning, stirring frequently, until mixture turns a dark reddish brown, about 20 minutes.

Add wine and continue simmering 30 minutes longer.

    Transfer mixture to a stock pot. Add cold water to cover, herbs, and spices and place on high heat. Bring to a boil, reduce to a simmer, and skim surface for scum. Simmer, uncovered, approximately 5 hours. Use as required or freeze for later use.

Fish Fumet

▶Special equipment:
*Non-oxidizing (stainless
steel or enamelled) stock pot
(otherwise the fumet will
turn cloudy).*

2 lbs./1 kg fish bones (preferably from flat saltwater
    species such as turbot, sole, or flounder)
4 cups/950 mL cold water
2 cups/480 mL white wine

FOR THE BOUQUET GARNI:
1 stalk celery, washed

1 leek, white only, washed
1 Spanish onion, split crosswise
6 white peppercorns, crushed
1 sprig fresh dill
1 sprig fresh tarragon
   or
1/4 tsp./1 mL dried tarragon

▶Yields 6 cups/1.5 litres
Place all ingredients in stock pot and bring to
a boil. Reduce to a simmer and cook, uncovered, 45 minutes.

Strain liquid through cheesecloth and discard
everything else. (Will keep in refrigerator two to
three days and can be frozen indefinitely.)

Marinated Salmon

4 lbs./2 kg salt

4 lbs./2 kg sugar

1 bunch pickling dill (usually available in late summer) or regular dill, roughly chopped

Equal amount fresh cilantro, roughly chopped

1 tsp./5 mL black peppercorns, crushed

1 Tbsp./15 mL coriander seeds, crushed

4-lb./2-kg whole salmon, trimmed and filleted

Olive oil to partially cover

▶ Special equipment:
Plastic or stainless steel container long enough to hold salmon fillets.

▶ Yields approximately 4 lbs./2 kg

Combine salt and sugar. Mix in herbs and spices. Sprinkle about one-third of mixture into container. Lay in one salmon fillet, skin side down, and cover completely with another third of mixture. Cover container with plastic wrap and refrigerate 24 hours, or let rest in a cool place (such as a basement) 12 to 16 hours.

Scrape marinade off fillets and put them back in container. Pour in enough olive oil to partially cover. Cover container and store in refrigerator. (Will keep up to 10 days.)

Gustav Partch's kitchen in Davos Dorf.

Mayonnaise

▶Tarragon variation:
Chop three sprigs fresh tarragon very finely and add to mayonnaise.

2 egg yolks
1 Tbsp./15 mL Dijon mustard
Juice of 1 lemon

¹/₄ cup/60 mL white wine vinegar
2 cups/480 mL sunflower oil
Salt and cayenne pepper to taste

▶Yields 2 cups/480 mL

Combine yolks, mustard, half the lemon juice, and half the vinegar in a stainless steel bowl and whisk briefly. Place bowl on a wet tea towel (to hold it in place) and, whisking constantly, pour in the oil in a steady stream.

Approximately halfway through, add remaining vinegar and lemon juice, salt, and cayenne. Add the rest of the oil. If consistency is too thick, whisk in about 1 Tbsp./15 mL warm water.

Michael Stadtländer at Scaramouche.

Crème Anglaise

4 cups/950 mL homogenized milk
1 cup/240 g sugar
10 egg yolks

¹/₄ cup/60 mL cold 35% whipping cream
1 vanilla bean, split lengthwise and scooped out
2 capfuls pure vanilla extract

▶ Vanilla ice cream:
Freeze crème anglaise mixture in a sorbétière.

▶ Yields 6 cups/1.5 litres

Combine the milk and sugar in a saucepan and scald. Remove from heat and whisk in egg yolks all at once. Return to low heat and stir constantly with a wooden spoon until thickened enough to coat the back of the spoon (about the consistency of house paint). Strain into a mixing bowl. Add cream and vanillas.

Use as required or keep in refrigerator up to one week.

Crème Fraîche

4 cups/950 mL 35% whipping cream
Juice of 1 lemon

¹/₂ cup/120 mL yogourt

▶ Sweet variation:
Add three capfuls pure vanilla extract and ¹/₂ cup/ 120 mL granulated sugar to mixture before leaving it to sit.

▶ Yields 4 cups/1 litre

Combine all ingredients in a stainless steel bowl. Cover with a clean cloth and leave at room temperature for 36 hours.

Transfer thickened cream to clean glass jars and refrigerate. (Will keep in refrigerator one week.)

Sugar Syrup

4 cups/950 mL water

2 lbs./1 kg sugar

▶ Yields 4 cups/950 mL

Combine sugar and water in a saucepan and bring to a boil.

Cook 5 minutes at a rolling boil. Remove from heat and cool before using.

Crepes

▶ Special equipment:
One or more 8-inch/20-cm nonstick crepe pans.

8 eggs
1 1/4 cups/300 mL all purpose flour
Salt to taste

1/4 tsp./1 mL freshly grated nutmeg
1/2 cup/120 mL melted butter
4 cups/950 mL milk

▶ Yields 18 to 20, 8-inch/20-cm crepes

Combine eggs, flour, salt, and nutmeg. Add melted butter. Add milk and combine well. Let batter rest at least 1 hour before cooking (it should be just thick enough to coat the back of a spoon).

Place crepe pan(s) over medium heat. Grease with butter (after the first crepes, this step shouldn't be necessary). Ladle in enough batter to coat bottom of pan thinly and cook 2 minutes. Turn and cook 1 minute longer. Slip crepe onto a wax-papered tray to cool.

Use right away or cool thoroughly, stack, and freeze.

Génoise

1 cup/240 mL sugar
8 large eggs
Grated rind of 1 lemon

$^7/_8$ cup/210 mL unsalted butter
2$^1/_2$ cups/600 mL sifted cake flour

▶Yields 1, 9-inch/22.5-cm cake
Preheat an oven to 375°F/190°C. Grease and flour a 9-inch/22.5-cm springform pan.

Combine sugar, eggs, and lemon rind in a stainless steel bowl. Whisk over a simmering bain-marie until frothy and slightly warmer than body temperature.

Transfer to another bowl and beat at high speed with an electric mixer until bowl feels cool to the touch.

Meanwhile, melt butter and keep warm but not hot.

Sift flour and fold into egg mixture with a rubber spatula, scraping sides of bowl. Fold in melted butter (do not overblend, or cake will lose height—you are relying on the beaten eggs for leavening). Pour batter into prepared pan and bake approximately 45 minutes.

Cool in pan 1 hour. Turn out and place on a rack until completely cool.

Cover with plastic wrap and store in refrigerator up to one week (for longer storage, use the freezer).

▶Chocolate variation:
Follow the above recipe with these changes:

Reduce sifted cake flour to 2 cups/475 mL and sift it again with 1$^1/_3$ cups/320 mL cocoa powder.

Reduce butter to $^2/_3$ cups/160 mL.

Choux Pastry

1 1/4 cups/300 mL skim milk

2/3 cup/160 mL unsalted butter

3 cups/720 mL sifted pastry flour

2 1/2 tsp./12 mL salt

2 Tbsp./30 mL sugar

1/4 cup/60 mL light rum

6 whole eggs

▶Yields approximately 2 lbs./1 kg

Place milk and butter in a saucepan and bring to a boil. Add flour and remove from heat. Then add salt and sugar and blend with a wooden spoon.

Return pan to heat and continue beating until dough forms a mass that pulls away from bottom and sides of pan.

Place dough in a bowl and beat with an electric mixer on slow speed, adding egg yolks one at a time and waiting until each one is fully absorbed before adding the next. Beat in rum.

Cover dough and store in refrigerator until ready to use. (Will keep one week.)

Puff Pastry

3$\frac{1}{2}$ cups/840 mL all purpose flour

1 cup/240 mL soft unsalted butter

1 Tbsp./15 mL salt

$\frac{7}{8}$ cup/200 mL cold water

1 cup/240 mL cold unsalted butter

▶ Yields approximately 2 lbs./1 kg

Sift flour and cut in first quantity of butter until pieces are no larger than peas. Combine salt and water and add to flour mixture.

Knead just until dough is homogeneous—do not overwork.

Form into a ball and cross-hatch the top $\frac{1}{2}$ inch/12 mm deep. Cover and refrigerate 1 hour.

On a lightly floured surface roll dough into a rectangle about $\frac{1}{3}$ inch/12 mm thick. Pull remaining butter into small pieces and arrange over two-thirds of dough. Beginning with unbuttered end, fold dough into thirds. Turn dough a quarter turn, so the fold is on the bottom, and roll again into a rectangle. Cover and refrigerate for 30 minutes.

Repeat this step four more times.

Puff pastry is now ready to use. (Will keep in refrigerator only overnight; for longer storage, use freezer.)

Pie Pastry

7 cups/1.75 litres sifted pastry flour
Salt to taste
1 lb./455 g cold unsalted butter

1 cup/240 mL cold water
1 Tbsp./15 mL brown sugar

▶ Yields approximately 2 lbs./1 kg

Sift flour and salt into a large mixing bowl. Cut butter in small cubes and work into flour by hand until texture resembles that of meal (do not overwork). Add water and sugar all at once and knead by hand until ingredients are well combined (again, do not overwork).

Form dough into a log and refrigerate at least 2 hours before rolling.

Use as required or freeze in single-use packages.

Sweet Pastry

10 cups/2.5 litres sifted pastry flour
2 1/8 cups/500 mL unsalted butter
3 eggs

1 capful pure vanilla extract
1 1/3 cups/320 mL granulated sugar

▶ Yields approximately 2 lbs./1 kg

Work flour and butter together as for pie pastry above. Beat together eggs, vanilla, and sugar and add to flour mixture all at once.

Knead dough until smooth. Refrigerate at least 2 hours before rolling.

Use as required or freeze in single-use packages.

Chocolate Wafer Batter

7 tsp./40 mL butter

3 Tbsp./45 mL sugar

1 Tbsp./15 mL cocoa powder

3 Tbsp./45 mL all purpose flour

3 Tbsp./45 mL egg whites

Pinch of salt

▶ Yields 18, 3-inch/7.5-cm wafers

Cream the butter and sugar together and beat with a wooden spoon for 5 minutes. Sift the cocoa powder and flour together. Add the sifted flour and the egg whites alternately and gradually until the batter is smooth. Refrigerate for 60 minutes before use.

This is a versatile chocolate-flavored crunchy wafer that can be formed into various shapes. You can freeze unused batter for another time.

Vanilla Wafer Batter

4 Tbsp./60 mL sugar

4 Tbsp./60 mL unsalted butter

$1/2$ vanilla bean, scraped

4 Tbsp./60 mL pastry flour, sifted

4 Tbsp./60 mL egg whites

Pinch of salt

▶ Yields 18, 3-inch/7.5-cm wafers

Cream the sugar, butter, and vanilla in a stainless steel bowl. Alternate adding the flour and the egg whites. Add the salt and mix to a smooth paste. Refrigerate for 60 minutes before use.

Pasta Dough

This is a standard pasta dough. I learned it from an Italian pastry chef in Switzerland. It works well for all rolled pasta shapes.

8 eggs
2 cups/480 mL all purpose flour
2 cups/480 mL fine ground semolina

1 Tbsp./15 mL fine olive oil
1 Tbsp./15 mL white wine vinegar
1 Tbsp./15 mL salt

Combine all ingredients in a stainless steel bowl. Knead the dough vigorously for 10 minutes. Allow the dough to rest at room temperature for 60 minutes before use.

Strudel Dough

This dough can be used for any pulled strudel recipe, either savoury or sweet. It is a German recipe given to me by my friend Michael Stadtländer.

1 1/2 cups/360 mL all purpose flour
3/4 cup/180 mL water
1 tsp./5 mL fresh lemon juice

3 Tbsp./45 mL melted unsalted butter
Pinch of salt

▶ Yields 1 dessert or 2 hors d'oeuvres strudel

Combine all the ingredients in a stainless steel bowl. Transfer the dough to a smooth surface for kneading. Knead the dough vigorously for 10 minutes or until the texture of the dough becomes satiny smooth. Cover the dough with plastic wrap and allow to rest for 4 hours at room temperature before use.

Spring

Russel Cottam at Scaramouche.

Shrimp and Swiss Chard Roll

This is an interesting hors d'oeuvre. It works well with an Off Dry Riesling. Pastis is a French aperitif that has a pronounced anise flavor. The combination works well and is traditional in French Mediterranean cuisine.

¹/₂ cup/120 mL fresh scallops

2 ice cubes

Salt to taste

1 egg yolk

1 tsp./5 mL pastis

1 Tbsp./15 mL soft butter

1 Tbsp./15 mL 35% whipping cream

2 washed Swiss chard leaves

6 large peeled and deveined shrimp

▶ Serves six

Place the scallops, ice, and salt in the food processor bowl and process. While processing, add the egg yolk, pastis, and butter. Add the cream in a slow, steady stream.

Bring a pot of water to the boil. Blanch the Swiss chard leaves for 30 seconds in the boiling water. Remove the leaves and pat dry with paper towels. Place some of the scallop mousse along the center of each chard leaf. Press the shrimps into the scallop mousse. Place more mousse on the shrimps. Wrap the chard leaves around the mousse and transfer to a vegetable steamer. Steam for 5 minutes. The scallop mousse is ready when it has set. (It will be firm to the touch.)

Slice the chard rolls across into 1-inch/ 2.5-cm pieces. Place them on a serving platter and serve warm.

Steve catering a wedding on board the Seguin.

Filled Morel on Apple Splinter

FOR THE CHICKEN MOUSSE:

$^1/_4$ lb./113 g boneless chicken breast

2 ice cubes

1 egg yolk

Salt and freshly ground black pepper to taste

1 Tbsp./15 mL soft butter

2 Tbsp./30 mL 35% whipping cream

$^1/_4$ cup/60 mL fresh green peas

12 whittled splinters of apple wood

FOR THE MORELS:

12 fresh morels

This is an hors d'oeuvre that can be served only in the spring because that's when the morels come out. Their honeycombed conical shape is unmistakable. Their flavor is considered among the most delicious of all wild mushrooms.

▶ Serves six

Roughly dice the chicken breast. Transfer the chicken to a food processor with the ice cubes. Turn on the machine and, while it is running, add the egg yolk and seasonings. Continue to process and add the butter and cream in a slow, steady stream.

Fold the peas into the chicken mousse. Fill each morel through the stem opening with the pea mixture. It is a tedious task, but a worthwhile effort.

Set a vegetable steamer on the stove. When the water is boiling, steam the filled morels for 2 minutes. Remove the morels and skewer each one through the stem end with an apple-wood splinter. The mousse should be set enough to hold the splinter securely.

Presentation:

Decorate a small platter with fresh green leaves or apple blossoms. Nestle the filled morels among the leaves. Serve at once.

Asparagus in Wild Rice Crepe
with Acidulated Wild Leeks

Here is a recipe that combines some of spring's offerings in a light first course or lunch dish. Use local asparagus.

FOR THE CREPES:

1 recipe Crepe Batter (page 20)

3 Tbsp./45 mL ground wild rice

FOR THE ASPARAGUS:

42 stalks asparagus, peeled and snapped

2 Tbsp./30 mL butter

1 tsp./5 mL roughly chopped fresh tarragon

6 bulbs wild leeks, cut into brunoise

   or

2 peeled shallots, cut into brunoise

1 Tbsp./15 mL white wine vinegar

▶ Serves six

Prepare the crepe batter following the directions, but substitute the ground wild rice for 3 Tbsp./45 mL of the flour. After letting the batter rest for 1 hour, make six crepes using a nonstick 8-inch/20-cm frying pan. Reserve.

Bring a large pot of salted water to the boil. If you are fortunate enough to own an asparagus steamer, by all means use it; otherwise the pot of boiling water will do fine.

When I say "snap" the asparagus, I mean to break the stems rather than cut them. I find they look too uniform in their presentation if they are all lined up like pencils in a pencil case. Snap the asparagus to a length of approximately 8 inches/20 cm. Cook the asparagus until they are tender. Bendy, but not mushy, asparagus is the ticket.

Toss the cooked asparagus in a bowl with the butter, tarragon, wild leeks or shallots, and vinegar.

Presentation:

Make a bundle of seven stalks of asparagus with herb-shallot mixture and place it inside each crepe. Roll the crepe around the asparagus. Place one crepe bundle on each of six plates and serve at once.

Wild Leek Tartlet

1 lb./455 g Pie Pastry (page 24)

FOR THE FILLING:

12 wild leeks, whole, washed

3 eggs
1 cup/240 mL 10% cream
Salt and freshly ground black pepper to taste

This dish is perfect with a salad for a delightful spring lunch. The leaves as well as the bulb of the wild leek are used. Use individual tartlet forms. I prefer the ones with the removable base and the scalloped sides that can be purchased at a kitchen supply store.

▶Serves six

Preheat an oven to 350°F/175°C. Roll out the pie dough to a ⅛-inch/.3-cm thickness. Cut rounds approximately 1 inch/2.5 cm wider than the diameter of the tartlet forms. Fit the pie dough into every nook and cranny of the tartlet forms. Fill each form with baking beans and blind bake until golden brown. Remove the baking beans from the forms.

Bring a saucepan of water to the boil. Trim the green leaves from the bulbs of the wild leeks. Cook the leaves in the boiling water for 5 minutes. Remove them and squeeze out excess cooking water. Transfer the cooked leaves to a blender. Purée and reserve.

Mix the eggs with the cream and seasonings in a stainless steel bowl. Add the purée of green wild leek. Slice the wild leek bulbs as thinly as possible on the bias. Place the baked tart forms on a baking sheet. Distribute the sliced wild leek bulbs among the tart forms. Pour some egg mixture into each form. Slide the tray into the oven and bake until the mixture puffs up and sets.

Serve the tartlet hot on its own or with a salad.

New Potato Crisps with Arctic Char Roe

*T*his is a dainty hors d'oeuvre. Any kind of roe could be substituted for Arctic char roe; salmon or whitefish might be easier to find. If you really feel like splurging, then Russian or Iranian caviar is what you want. The combination of fish eggs with potato is a good one, and the crème fraîche mollifies the salty fishiness.

6 peeled new potatoes
2 cups/480 mL sunflower oil
Salt to taste

$^1/_2$ cup/120 mL Crème Fraîche (page 19)
2 Tbsp./30 mL Arctic char roe

▶Serves six

Use a mandolin to slice the potatoes thinly. Cut the slices in julienne. Pour the sunflower oil into a soup pot and bring the temperature to 250°F/120°C. Add the potato julienne and blanch for 30 seconds. Remove the julienne to a plate. While the potatoes are still warm, fashion 12 free-form bite-sized nests of potato. Increase the temperature of the oil to 350°F/175°C. Fry the potato nests to a golden crisp.

Remove to paper towels to drain. Season the crisps with salt. Place a dab of crème fraîche on each crisp. Spoon some roe directly on the crème fraîche.

Serve at once as a canapé with sparkling wine.

Wild Leek Soup with Morels à la Crème

FOR THE SOUP:

2 Tbsp./30 mL butter

1 Spanish onion, peeled and sliced

1 leek, cleaned and sliced

2 Yukon Gold potatoes, peeled and sliced

1 bay leaf

Salt and freshly ground black pepper to taste

8 cups/2 litres Chicken Stock (page 14)

  or

Tomato Consommé (page 14)

12 wild leeks, cleaned (greens only)

FOR THE GARNISH:

2 Tbsp./30 mL butter

2 Yukon Gold potatoes, peeled and cut into dice

12 wild leeks (whites only), cut into brunoise

Salt and freshly ground black pepper to taste

FOR THE MORELS À LA CRÈME:

2 Tbsp./30 mL butter

18 whole morels

Salt and freshly ground black pepper to taste

$1/4$ cup/60 mL whipped 35% whipping cream

▶ Serves six

Melt the butter for the soup and add the vegetables. Gently sauté for 5 minutes. Add the bay leaf, seasonings, stock or consommé, and simmer, covered, for 45 minutes. Purée in a food processor. Reserve.

In a separate pot bring 8 cups/2 litres of water to the boil.

Cook the wild leek greens in the boiling water for 5 minutes. Squeeze out excess water from the cooked greens and transfer them to a blender. Purée and reserve.

Preheat an oven to 325°F/165°C. Melt the butter for the garnish in a frying pan. Add the diced potatoes and the brunoise of wild leek bulbs. Season with salt and pepper. Cover with foil or a snugly fitting lid and bake for 30 minutes or until the potatoes are steamed tender. Reserve.

Heat the butter for the morels in a frying pan. Add the morels and the seasonings. Gently sauté for 5 minutes until the morels soften. Reserve.

Presentation:

Warm six soup bowls. Spoon some potato and wild leek mixture into each bowl. Bring the soup to the boil and whisk in the wild leek purée. Ladle some soup into each bowl. Spoon the whipped cream into the sautéed morels and fold in. Place a dollop of the creamy morels in the center of each soup bowl. Serve at once.

Chilled Salmon Tartare Soup

FOR THE SOUP BASE:

1 Spanish onion, peeled and sliced

1 leek, cleaned and sliced

1 fennel bulb, trimmed and sliced

1 celery root, peeled and sliced

1 potato, peeled and sliced

10 cups/2.5 litres Chicken Stock (page 14)

1 bay leaf

12 whole peppercorns

1 sprig of fresh tarragon

Salt to taste

FOR THE GARNISH:

2 cooked potatoes, diced

FOR THE TARTARE:

$^1/_2$ lb./227 g fresh salmon, very finely diced

1 tsp./5mL finely chopped dill

1 tsp./5mL peeled shallot, cut into brunoise

1 tsp./5mL finely chopped capers

Salt and freshly ground black pepper to taste

TO FINISH THE SOUP:

1 cup/240 mL plain yogourt

▶ Serves six

Put a large soup pot on the stove and add all the soup base ingredients. Bring to the boil and simmer for 1 hour. Purée the soup in a food processor and pass through a fine sieve. Refrigerate overnight; it will keep for two days.

On the day that you wish to serve the soup, prepare the potatoes and reserve at room temperature. Combine all the ingredients for the tartare. Season strongly with salt and pepper.

Presentation:

Chill six soup bowls. Spoon some potato dice into each bowl. Mix together the soup, tartare, and yogourt. Taste and adjust for seasoning. If the soup is too thick, adjust with water. Serve cold.

Morel Consommé under Puff Pastry

FOR THE CONSOMMÉ CLARIFICATION:

1 small Spanish onion, cut in rough dice

2 cloves garlic, roughly chopped

1 leek, cleaned and roughly chopped

1 celery root, scrubbed and roughly chopped

1 quart/litre jar Tomato Sauce (page 156)

2 lbs./900 g fresh morels

1 tbsp./15 mL roughly chopped fresh thyme

12 cracked black peppercorns

$^{1}/_{2}$ tsp./2.5 mL freshly grated nutmeg

2 bay leaves

2 whole cloves

6 egg whites

12 cups/3 litres Chicken Stock (page 14)

FOR THE GARNISH:

18 small fresh morels

3 Tbsp./45 mL leek julienne

FOR THE PASTRY:

1 lb./455 g Puff Pastry (page 23) or frozen

1 beaten egg

Here is a dish that looks spectacular when it is presented. Paul Bocuse made this style of presentation famous with his truffle soup. You break through the dome of golden flaky pastry and immediately your senses are assailed with the warm, earthy aroma of forest mushrooms. In this case they are morels and they are one of spring's treasures.

▶ Serves six

Place all the ingredients for the clarification, except the chicken stock, in a large, thick-bottomed soup pot. Mix thoroughly with your hand to disperse the egg whites. Add the chicken stock and mix thoroughly again. Place on low heat and nurse to a boil, stirring often. As the clarification nears the boiling point a raft will begin to form on the surface. This is made up of the soup ingredients bound by the egg whites as they coagulate with the heat. It is important not to stir the consommé once the raft has formed. Rather, let it slowly boil and percolate through the raft to clarify the liquid. This percolation will infuse the flavors into a distillate redolent of morels. This process will take 1 hour. Strain the liquid through a cheese-cloth-lined strainer. Refrigerate for 3 hours.

Place some leek julienne and three morels into each of six steep-sided ovenproof soup bowls. Pour chilled consommé until each bowl is two-thirds full. Reserve.

Preheat an oven to 350°F/175°C. Roll puff pastry out to a thickness of $^{1}/_{4}$ inch/.6 cm. Cut rounds of dough large enough to drape over the bowls of soup with a $^{1}/_{2}$-inch/1.2-cm overhang all around. Use a pastry brush to paint beaten egg around the edge and side of each bowl. Drape a round of pastry over each bowl. Lightly press the overhang into the eggwash to hold the pastry in place. Lightly paint the surface of the pastry with beaten egg. Place the bowls in the oven for 15 minutes or until a golden dome of pastry has risen above each bowl. Remove the bowls and serve at once.

Green Pea Soup with Lettuce

The day that you harvest the first peas from your garden or purchase the first peas from the market is the day to make this soup. Success depends on the sweet freshness of the peas.

FOR THE SOUP:

2 Tbsp./30 mL butter

2 shallots, peeled and cut into brunoise

2 Tbsp./30 mL smoked ham, cut into brunoise

2 cups/480 mL fresh green peas

8 cups/2 litres Chicken Stock (page 14)
Salt and freshly ground black pepper to taste

FOR THE GARNISH:

6 leaves of Boston or butter lettuce, washed

3 Tbsp./45 mL blanched fresh green peas

1 basil leaf, cut into julienne

▶ Serves six

Melt the butter in a soup pot over low heat. Add the shallot and ham brunoise. Gently sauté for 5 minutes. Add the peas and chicken stock. Cook for 5 minutes or until the peas are tender. Transfer to a blender or food processor to purée. Reserve.

Set a vegetable steamer on the stove. Steam the lettuce leaves briefly until they are wilted.

Cut the leaves into julienne. Mix with the peas and the basil julienne.

Presentation:

Warm six soup bowls in the oven. Remove them and place an equal amount of garnish in each bowl. Fill each bowl with soup. Grind some black pepper on top. Serve at once.

Chicken and Watercress Soup

FOR THE SOUP:

2 lbs./900 g coarsely ground chicken leg meat

1 Spanish onion, roughly chopped

1 leek, cleaned and roughly chopped

1 celery root, scrubbed and roughly chopped

1 carrot, peeled and roughly chopped

12 cracked black peppercorns

2 bay leaves

1 Tbsp./15 mL roughly chopped fresh rosemary

Salt to taste

6 egg whites

12 cups/3 litres Chicken Stock (page 14)

FOR THE GARNISH:

1 Tbsp./15 mL fresh ginger root, peeled and cut into julienne

6 sprigs of watercress

1/2 boneless skinless chicken breast

This soup has a distinct Asian feel. The combination of chicken, ginger, and watercress evokes childhood memories of first-time dining experiences in Chinese restaurants.

▶ Serves six

Put all the soup ingredients, except the chicken stock, in a large, heavy-bottomed soup pot. Mix thoroughly by hand. Allow the soup to percolate for 2 hours and pass the liquid through a cheesecloth-lined strainer. Reserve.

Cut the chicken breast into six equal pieces. Pound the pieces as thinly as possible between two sheets of plastic.

Presentation:

Warm six soup bowls. Place some ginger julienne, some watercress leaves, and one slice of pounded chicken breast in each bowl. Ladle boiling consommé over the garnish to cook the chicken. Serve at once.

Palmerston construction.

Sorrel Soup

Sorrel is a hardy spring herb. It has a unique sour taste that is refreshing in a soup.

FOR THE SOUP:

3 Tbsp./45 mL butter

1 Spanish onion, peeled and sliced

2 potatoes, peeled and sliced

12 fresh sorrel leaves

2 bay leaves

6 cracked black peppercorns

8 cups/2 litres Chicken Stock (page 14)

Salt to taste

FOR THE GARNISH:

3 Tbsp./45 mL Crème Fraîche (page 19)

2 sorrel leaves, cut into julienne

▶ Serves six

Melt the butter in a soup pot. Add the onions and gently sauté for 5 minutes. Add the rest of the soup ingredients and simmer for 30 minutes or until the potatoes are tender. Purée in a food processor.

Presentation:

Warm six soup bowls. Pour soup into each bowl. Place a dollop of crème fraîche and a sprinkling of sorrel julienne on top of the crème fraîche in each bowl. Serve at once.

Michael Pawlick in Palmerston Garden.

Dover Sole Paupiettes in Provençal Bouillon

FOR THE BOUILLON:

2 whole Dover sole

8 sea scallops

³/₄ bulb fennel, cleaned and cut into rough dice

1 Spanish onion, cut into rough dice

1 celery root, scrubbed and cut into rough dice

1 leek, cleaned and sliced

3 cloves garlic, sliced

¹/₄ tsp./1.2 mL saffron

¹/₄ tsp./1.2 mL dried lavender

¹/₄ tsp./1.2 mL orange zest

4 egg whites

1 cup/240 mL Tomato Sauce (page 156)

2 cups/480 mL Chicken Stock (page 14)

1, 25-oz. /750-mL bottle unoaked Chardonnay wine

Salt to taste

FOR THE GARNISH:

1 Tbsp./15 mL orange zest, cut into julienne

2 Tbsp./30 mL fennel cut into julienne

12 strands of saffron

▶ Serves six

Fillet the fish. Each fish has four fillets, so you will have a total of eight fillets when you've finished. Refrigerate the fillets and the scallops. Chop the bones of the fish and set them in a large, heavy-bottomed soup pot. Add the rest of the soup ingredients, except for the chicken stock and the wine. Mix thoroughly by hand to incorporate the egg whites. Add the chicken stock, wine, and salt. Mix thoroughly again. Place the pot on low heat and nurse to the boil, stirring regularly. Once the raft forms, percolate for 45 minutes and pass through a cheesecloth-lined strainer. Reserve.

Take the fillets out of the refrigerator. Lay the fish on the counter with the whiter side of the fillet facing down. Pound the fillets gently with the heel of a saucepan to flatten them as much as possible without breaking the flesh. Place a scallop in the wider end of each fillet, roll the fillet around it, and secure with a toothpick or small wooden skewer.

Set a vegetable steamer on the stove. When the water is boiling, steam the paupiettes for 4 minutes or until the sole has turned an opaque white. While the paupiettes are steaming, bring the Provençal bouillon back to a simmer.

Presentation:

Warm six soup bowls. Place an equal amount of garnish in each bowl. Cut each paupiette in half across the middle. Place the two halves, with the exposed scallop facing up, in each bowl. Ladle bouillon into each bowl. Serve at once.

The inspiration for this dish came from trying to capture, in a clear broth form, some of the typical flavors of Provençe. It was in the context of a multi-coursed dinner that this dish was conceived so it needed to be intensely flavored but not too rich. Here it may be enjoyed as either a soup or a fish course.

Dover sole is devilishly expensive, as it should be, because it has been fished practically into commercial extinction. The thing is, though, that no other fish works as well.

Chive Cream Soup

Chives are one of the first things to push through the earth in spring. This soup is a celebration of chives.

FOR THE SOUP:

3 Tbsp./45 mL unsalted butter

1 Spanish onion, peeled and sliced

2 potatoes, peeled and sliced

2 cups/480 mL Chicken Stock (page 14)

Salt to taste

1 cup/240 mL roughly cut chives

▶ Serves six

Melt the butter in a large soup pot. Add the onion and gently sauté for 5 minutes. Add the potatoes and the chicken stock. Season with salt. Cook for 30 minutes or until the potatoes are tender. Transfer to a blender. While the blender is running, add the chives. Pass through a fine sieve.

FOR THE GARNISH:

3 Tbsp./45 mL Crème Fraîche (page 19)

Freshly ground black pepper

2 Tbsp./30 mL finely sliced chives

Presentation:

Warm six soup bowls. Pour some soup into each bowl. Add a dollop of crème fraîche, a grinding of pepper, and a sprinkling of chives to each bowl. Serve at once.

Sautéed Dandelion Sandwiches

4 Tbsp./60 mL olive oil for cooking
2 cloves garlic, finely chopped
3 potatoes, cooked, peeled, and sliced
2 lbs./900 g young dandelion greens, washed

Salt and freshly ground black pepper to taste
2 Tbsp./30 mL lemon juice
12 slices buttered bread

▶ Serves six

Place a large frying pan on medium heat and add the oil and garlic. Add the potatoes and fry to golden brown on both sides. Add the dandelion leaves and sauté just long enough to wilt the leaves. Season with salt, pepper, and lemon juice.

When the dandelion mixture has cooled to room temperature, divide it to make each sandwich. Slice the sandwiches in half and serve.

Choose only the youngest sprouts of dandelion for this recipe. Dandelion is naturally a bitter green and as it grows it becomes even more bitter. The young leaves are delicious. A Greek woman named Potoula, who used to work with me, would sometimes bring these sandwiches from home. She called the green "chicoria." The inspiration for this recipe comes from her.

Palmerston Garden.

Green Pea Risotto

This is a great vegetarian dish on its own or as an accompaniment to lamb or lobster. The pea and basil combination is always pleasant.

2 Tbsp./60 mL olive oil for cooking

2 cloves garlic, split in half

2 cups/480 mL Italian risotto rice (Arborio or Vialone)

4 cups/950 mL Tomato Consommé (page 14)

1 bay leaf

2 cups/480 mL fresh green peas

1/2 cup/120 mL Vernaccia, or other dry Italian white wine

4 Tbsp./60 mL 35% whipping cream

1 cup/240 mL grated Parmigiano Reggiano

2 Tbsp./30 mL fresh basil, cut in chiffonade

▶ Serves six

Heat a large frying pan, then add the olive oil and garlic. "Toast" the rice in the oil over medium heat for 5 minutes or until the grains have a slightly golden hue. Warm the tomato consommé in a separate pot. Add the consommé in small amounts to the rice, stirring continuously. The idea here is to release surface starch in the rice by stirring. This is what will give the rice its creamy texture in the end.

Add the bay leaf and peas. Keep adding the consommé until it is all absorbed. Finish the risotto with the wine, cream, cheese, and basil. Make sure the cheese is completely integrated and melted into the rice. Serve at once.

Pascaline Phillips at Palmerston.

Ratatouille Gratin with Green Herb Crust

FOR THE GREEN HERB CRUST:

2 Tbsp./30 mL chopped Italian parsley

2 Tbsp./30 mL chopped fresh basil

1 cup/240 mL white crustless bread crumbs

FOR THE RATATOUILLE:

4 Tbsp./60 mL olive oil for cooking

2 cloves garlic, finely chopped

2 zucchinis, cleaned and cut into bite-sized pieces

1 eggplant, cleaned and cut into bite-sized pieces

1 Spanish onion, cut into bite-sized pieces

4 tomatoes, seeded and cut into bite-sized pieces

1 Tbsp./15 mL chopped basil

Salt and freshly ground black pepper to taste

▶ Serves six

Place the chopped herbs in a food processor. While the machine is running, pour in the breadcrumbs. Process until there is an even green color throughout. Reserve.

Preheat an oven to 350°F/175°C. Heat the oil in a large frying pan. Add the garlic. Sauté the zucchini, eggplant, and onion for 5 minutes.

Add the tomatoes, basil, and seasonings. Cover and simmer for 10 minutes. Transfer the vegetables to individual baking dishes or a large baking dish. Sprinkle liberally with the breadcrumb mixture. Bake for 15 minutes or until the breadcrumbs are golden brown. Serve at once.

I remember trying to find this dish in all my classic French cookery books, but none had any recipes for ratatouille. I was puzzled because it seemed like many restaurants had ratatouille on their menus. I have since learned that it is a regional dish from the south of France and, until fairly recently, had not been elevated to classic status. My interpretation has the addition of a green herb crust that gives a crunchy textural counterpoint to this quick stew of vegetables.

This dish can be made in individual ovenproof dishes or a large ceramic baking dish.

Creamy Polenta with Fresh Morels

There is something very comforting about polenta served in this way. The addition of morels gives the dish a seasonal context.

FOR THE POLENTA:

1 cup/240 mL Creamy Polenta (page 188)

FOR THE MORELS:

2 Tbsp./30 mL butter

2 shallots, peeled and cut into brunoise

1 lb./455 g fresh morels

1 tsp./5 mL fresh thyme leaves

1 tsp./5 mL chopped parsley

Salt and freshly ground black pepper to taste

▶Serves six

Prepare the creamy polenta and reserve. Place a large frying pan over medium heat. Melt the butter, then add the shallots and morels. Sauté for 5 minutes. Add the herbs and seasonings.

Presentation:

Warm six plates. Place some creamy polenta on each plate. Place an equal amount of sautéed morels directly on the polenta. Serve at once as an appetizer.

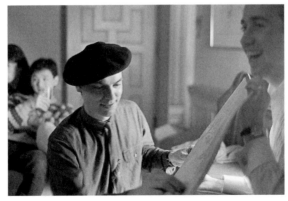

Richard d'Amours at Palmerston Christmas Party.

Asparagus with Classic Vinaigrette

FOR THE VINAIGRETTE:

2 egg yolks

2 tsp./10 mL Dijon mustard

1 tsp./5 mL white wine vinegar

1 tsp./5 mL fresh lemon juice

5 Tbsp./75 mL sunflower oil

Salt and freshly ground black pepper to taste

FOR THE ASPARAGUS:

42 peeled stalks of asparagus

FOR THE GARNISH:

1 hard boiled egg

2 shallots, peeled and cut into brunoise

3 Tbsp./45 mL Roasted Red Peppers (page 155), cut into brunoise

3 Tbsp./45 mL Italian parsley leaves, chopped

This is an attractive dish on a buffet because of its vibrant colors. It is easy to serve and delicious. It is also terrific as a plated appetizer. To help the vinaigrette to emulsify, it is important to have all the ingredients at room temperature.

▶ Serves six

Mix together the egg yolks, mustard, vinegar, and lemon juice in a stainless steel bowl. Slowly add the sunflower oil in a steady stream. Season with salt and pepper.

Separate the yolk from the white of the hard boiled egg and chop each finely. Keep all the garnishes in separate bowls. Reserve.

Snap the bases of the asparagus to leave 8 inches/20 cm of stalk. Steam or boil the asparagus until tender.

Presentation:

Pour a small pool of vinaigrette into the center of each plate. Place a bundle of seven stalks of cooked asparagus on each pool of vinaigrette. Garnish each bundle with a row of parsley, egg white, roasted pepper, shallot, and egg yolk. Serve at room temperature.

Roast Asparagus with Noisette Butter
and Sherry Vinegar

O ne usually thinks of asparagus as such a delicate and tender vegetable that when considering cooking it, steaming or simmering spring to mind. Recently, I have discovered that roasting or grilling asparagus also gives delicious results. I think it's possible that roasting might even give asparagus a more intense flavor because there is no water to leach flavor away. Also, when I roast the asparagus I don't peel it, so it is a less time-consuming cooking method.

The butter is called "noisette" because as the butter begins to caramelize it gives off a wonderful, rich, nutty aroma reminiscent of hazelnuts.

42 asparagus stalks, washed and snapped
8 Tbsp./120 mL butter
1 Tbsp./15 mL sherry vinegar

1 tsp./5 mL lemon juice
Salt and freshly ground black pepper to taste

▶Serves six

Preheat an oven to 450°F/230°C.

Spread out the asparagus on a baking sheet. Try not to crowd the stalks too much. Use two baking sheets if necessary. Place the trays in the oven.

Meanwhile, melt the butter over medium heat in a small saucepan. Watch the butter carefully after it has melted. It should foam up and boil rapidly. As the boiling subsides, the butter will begin to change color. As it does

this, remove the pot from the stove and add the vinegar and lemon juice.

Remove the asparagus from the oven after 8 minutes or when it is bendy, but not mushy.

Presentation:

Warm six plates. Spread seven stalks of cooked asparagus in a fan pattern on each plate. Spoon some of the butter mixture over the asparagus and serve at once.

New Year's Eve in the kitchen.

Boston Lettuce with Acidulated Wild Leeks
and Sorrel Dressing

FOR THE DRESSING:

1 egg yolk

1 tsp./5 mL Dijon mustard

1 Tbsp./15 mL white wine vinegar

6 sorrel leaves

6 Tbsp./120 mL sunflower oil

2 Tbsp./30 mL 35% whipping cream

Salt and freshly ground black pepper to taste

FOR THE ACIDULATED WILD LEEKS:

12 wild leek bulbs, cleaned and cut into brunoise

2 Tbsp./30 mL white wine vinegar

FOR THE LETTUCE:

2 heads Boston lettuce leaves, washed

▶ Serves six

Place the egg yolk in a blender. Add the mustard and the white wine vinegar. Chop the sorrel leaves and, while the motor is running, add the sorrel leaves to the blender. Trickle the sunflower oil in, in a steady stream. Add the whipping cream. Season with salt and pepper. Reserve.

Place the brunoise of wild leek bulbs in a small ceramic or stainless steel bowl with the vinegar. Reserve.

Presentation:

Chill six plates. Toss the lettuce leaves with the sorrel dressing and mound the leaves in a pile on each plate. Garnish with a sprinkling of wild leek brunoise. Serve at once.

New Potato and Oka Melt with Pickled Beets

The pickled beets cut through the richness of the cheese in this dish. It is perfect for lunch or as a savoury after the main course in a multi-course dinner.

18 small new potatoes
1 lb./455g Oka cheese
1 quart/litre jar Pickled Beets (page 115)
   or
6 small golden beets and 6 candycane beets

2 Tbsp./30 mL white wine vinegar
1 shallot, peeled and cut into brunoise
Salt and freshly ground black pepper to taste

▶ Serves six

Preheat an oven to 350°F/175°C. Cook the new potatoes in boiling salted water. If you are using fresh beets, cook them in boiling salted water. If they are very small, they will take approximately the same amount of time as the potatoes. When the vegetables are cooked, drain them and let them cool. When the potatoes are cool enough to handle, cut them in half and place six halves facing up in the center of six ovenproof plates. Slice six wedges of cheese and place one wedge on each mound of potatoes. Place the plates in the oven. If using fresh beets, peel and slice the beets into quarters. While they are still warm, toss them in a marinade of the vinegar, shallots, and seasoning.

Remove the plates from the oven when the cheese has melted. Garnish each plate with five quarters of marinated beets or pickled beets. (The leftover marinated beets keep very well in the refrigerator.) Serve at once.

Facing page: Poached Arctic Char with Court Bouillon Vegetables and Sorrel Beurre Blanc (page 54)
Following page: Filled Morel on Apple Splinter (page 29)

Poached Trout with Wild Leek Mignonette

FOR THE COURT BOUILLON:

2 quarts/2 litres water

1 medium onion, sliced

1 carrot, peeled and sliced

1 celery stalk, cleaned and sliced

1 leek, cleaned and sliced

2 Tbsp./30 mL white wine vinegar

Salt to taste

1 bay leaf

15 whole black peppercorns

1 sprig of dill

FOR THE MIGNONETTE:

6 whole wild leeks, cleaned

3 Tbsp./45 mL white wine vinegar

Freshly ground black pepper to taste

Salt to taste

6 small fresh rainbow trout fillets, pin bones removed

▶Serves six

To prepare the court bouillon, boil the water in a stainless steel pot. Add the sliced vegetables, vinegar, and seasonings. Cook for 5 minutes. Reduce the heat to a simmer.

Meanwhile, prepare the mignonette. Finely dice the wild leeks, stems, and leaves together. Add the vinegar and black pepper. Season with salt. Reserve.

Simmer the trout fillets in the court bouillon for 5 minutes. The flesh should just be opaque. Do not overcook.

Presentation:

Remove the fillets with a slotted spoon and place them skin side up on six plates. Peel the skin back to expose the fillet underneath. Place some of the court bouillon vegetables around the fillet. Spoon some of the mignonette on each fillet. Serve with boiled new potatoes.

You can buy fresh trout fillets in many parts of North America at any time of the year. I like to think that they are best in spring because that is when the trout fishing season opens and the rivers are full of them. I have seen them jumping in the Ganaraska River in Port Hope, Ontario, and have caught the rich aroma of maple sap boiling on the wind from a nearby sugar shack at the same time. Venture into the woods farther back from the stream and you will probably find wild leeks springing up everywhere.

Facing page: Baked Rhubarb Tart with Marzipan Sauce
(page 61)

Previous page: Wild Leek Soup with Morels à la Crème
(page 33)

Chilled Lobster with Chive Linguini
and Tomato Jelly

Late spring is when lobster season opens in the Maritimes. It's the time of year when lobsters are at their peak. This recipe calls for the smallest size of lobster, sometimes called "canner lobsters." These are lobsters that usually weigh around 8 oz./225 g each.

FOR THE JELLY:
3 cups/720 mL Tomato Consommé (page 14)
4 gelatin leaves

FOR THE LINGUINI:
4 oz./113 g linguini

18 whole chives
2 Tbsp./30 mL fine olive oil

FOR THE LOBSTER:
6 live canner or 1-lb./455-g lobsters

▶ Serves six

Warm the consommé in a stainless steel saucepan. Soak the gelatin leaves in cold water. Squeeze out the excess water and add the gelatin to the consommé. Stir the consommé just long enough to melt the gelatin. Refrigerate.

Cook the linguini in a large pot of rapidly boiling, salted water. Drain the linguini in a colander. Place the whole chives in a bowl with the fine olive oil and add the linguini. Toss to evenly distibute the oil and to wilt the chives. Reserve.

Cook the lobsters, one at a time, in a large pot of rapidly boiling, salted water. Allow 4 minutes for each lobster. When the lobsters are cool enough to handle, separate the claws from the body. Separate the tail from the body and, using a pair of scissors and cutting from underneath, slit the tail lengthwise and remove the tail meat in one piece. Remove the meat from each claw in one piece using a pair of nutcrackers and a skewer. Cut each tail into five pieces with a sharp knife.

Presentation:

Chill six bowls. Use a carving fork to wind up some linguini with chives. Place the linguini and chives in each bowl. Place the tail meat on the the linguini approximately where the tail would be on a whole lobster. Place the claws where they would be. Place two chives imitating antennae. Spoon some tomato jelly on both sides of the linguini. Serve at once.

Chili and Rock Salt Grilled Salmon

6, 6-oz./160-g fillets fresh salmon

2 green chilies, finely chopped

Coarse-grained salt to taste

▶ Serves six

Prepare a charcoal or gas barbeque. Coat the fillets of salmon with a paste of coarse-grained salt and chilies. Wait until the barbeque has burned down to a nice slow fire or set the gas barbeque to low heat. Place the fillets of salmon, skin side down, on the grill. Grill until each side is golden brown, about 7 minutes per side. Serve with steamed new potatoes and asparagus.

Clams Steamed in Lovage Broth

3 Tbsp./45 mL olive oil for cooking

2 cloves garlic, finely chopped

1 Tbsp./15 mL ham, cut into julienne

2 shallots, peeled and cut into brunoise

36 washed littleneck clams

1 cup/240 mL Chicken Stock (page 14)

1 cup/240 mL dry Riesling wine

2 Tbsp./30 mL washed and chopped lovage leaves

Salt and freshly ground black pepper to taste

Lovage is an herb that tastes like a cross between parsley and celery. It is a hardy perennial and is one of the first herbs to burst forth in spring.

▶ Serves six

Heat the olive oil in a large soup pot. Add the garlic, ham, and shallots. Sauté gently for 5 minutes. Add the clams. Add the stock and the wine. Bring to the boil and cover. Steam for 5 minutes or until the clams open.

Presentation:

Warm six bowls. Place six clams, with their open side facing up, in each bowl. Pour the cooking liquid into a blender. With the motor running, add the chopped lovage. Pour the blended broth into each soup bowl and serve at once.

Warm Lobster with Pea Risotto
and Coral Sauce

Coral sauce is lobster bisque with the addition of lobster coral (roe) at the last minute to add color and richness. In late spring you are much more likely to find lobsters containing their coral than at any other time of year. The coral is everywhere inside the lobster. It is green-black when raw and red-orange when cooked.

6, 1½-lb./680-g live lobsters
2 cups/480 mL Lobster Bisque (page 88)
1 Tbsp./30 mL raw lobster coral

1 recipe Green Pea Risotto (page 42)
12 chives

▶ Serves six

Bring a large soup pot of salted water to the boil. Cook the lobsters one at a time for 8 minutes each. Remove the lobsters with a slotted spoon and let them cool. Separate the shells from the meat.

Bring the bisque to a boil. Transfer the bisque to a blender and, while the motor is running, add the lobster coral and blend for a few seconds. Reserve.

Preheat an oven to 275°F/135°C. Prepare the green pea risotto. Slice the lobster tail into five slices preserving the form of the whole tail by keeping the slices in order. Carefully place the tails in a baking dish with the claws. Cover with aluminum foil and warm in the oven.

Presentation:

Warm six dinner plates. Place a long, oval mound of risotto in the center of each plate. Arrange the lobster tail in overlapping slices running the length of the mound. Arrange the claws to the right and left of the mound. Pour coral sauce on the plate. Garnish with two chives imitating antennae.

Fried Soft-Shell Crab with Piquant Sauce

FOR THE CRABS:

2 cups/480 mL sunflower oil

1 tsp./5 mL dried chili flakes

½ cup/120 mL all purpose flour

6 soft-shell crabs, eyes and gills removed

FOR THE SAUCE:

1 green chili, finely chopped

½ cup/120 mL Roasted Red Peppers (page 155)

1 Tbsp./15 mL white wine vinegar

Salt to taste

FOR THE SALAD:

2 cups/480 mL mixed salad greens

*O*rdinary blue crabs are nice to eat, but it is difficult to get fed because it takes so much time and work to get at the meat. When the crabs shed their hard shells and molt, as they do in the spring, they suddenly become a delicacy. Their entire body becomes edible, shell and all!

▶Serves six

Heat the sunflower oil in a soup pot on high heat. Reduce the oil to a simmer once the temperature reaches 350°F/175°C.

Sprinkle the chili flakes into a blender and, while the motor is running, add 3 Tbsp./45 mL flour. Mix this seasoned flour with another 3 Tbsp./45 mL flour. Dredge the crabs in this mixture. Fry the crabs one at a time in the oil for 3 minutes or until they redden. Remove them with a slotted spoon and drain them on paper towels.

Mix the chopped chili and the roasted red peppers in a blender. While the motor is running, add the vinegar and salt. Reserve.

Wash and spin the greens. Place a small mound on each of six plates. Place one fried crab on each mound of lettuce. Spoon some sauce on either side of the crab. Serve while the crab is still warm.

Roberta and Lloyd.

Poached Arctic Char
with Court Bouillon Vegetables and Sorrel Beurre Blanc

Sorrel is a spring peren-nial herb that is usually made into soup. I like the green acidic taste because it contrasts the rich mellow-ness of fresh Arctic char. Use Arctic char fillets for this recipe. Ask the fish-monger to cut servings that weigh 5 oz./150 g each.

FOR THE COURT BOUILLON:

8 cups/2 litres water

1 Spanish onion, peeled and sliced

1 carrot, scrubbed and sliced

1 celery stalk, washed and sliced

3 Tbsp./45 mL white wine vinegar

12 cracked black peppercorns

2 bay leaves

Salt to taste

FOR THE SAUCE:

1 cup/240 mL dry Riesling wine

1/2 cup/120 mL white wine vinegar

2 shallots, sliced

1 tsp./5 mL cracked black peppercorns

3 Tbsp./45 mL butter

12 fresh sorrel leaves

FOR THE GARNISH:

1 scrubbed carrot, sliced thinly and on the bias

1 washed leek, sliced thinly and on the bias

1 peeled celery root, sliced thinly and on the bias

6 fresh sorrel leaves, cut in chiffonade

12 small new potatoes, left whole

FOR THE ARCTIC CHAR:

6, 5-oz./150-g servings of fresh Arctic char fillet, pin bones removed

▶Serves six

Bring a large soup pot with the water to a boil. Add the court bouillon ingredients and simmer gently for 20 minutes. Reserve.

Place all the ingredients for the sauce, except the butter and the sorrel, in a saucepan to boil. When the liquid has reduced to a syrupy consistency, transfer it to a blender and blend. While the motor is running add the butter and sorrel. Strain and reserve the sauce.

Slice the vegetables finely and steam them until they are tender. Cook the potatoes in boil-ing salted water until they are tender. Slice the sorrel leaves into chiffonade.

Bring the court bouillon back to a simmer. Poach the Arctic char in the court bouillon for 5 minutes, or until flesh is opaque throughout.

Presentation:

Warm six plates. Arrange the garnish vegetables around the perimeter of each plate. Spoon some sorrel beurre blanc into the center of each plate. Place Arctic char on the sauce, skin side up.

Peel the skin back to expose some of the fish underneath it. Sprinkle each plate with sorrel chiffonade. Serve at once.

Seared Yogourt-Marinated Chicken Breast
with Fiddleheads

FOR THE CHICKEN:

2 Tbsp./30 mL whole cumin

1 Tbsp./15 mL whole coriander seed

1 tsp./5 mL whole black pepper

1 clove garlic, finely chopped

1 cup/240 mL plain yogourt

6 boneless skinless chicken breasts

Salt to taste

1 Tbsp./15 mL sunflower oil

FOR THE FIDDLEHEADS:

1 lb./455 g fresh fiddlehead ferns

1 Tbsp./15 mL butter

Salt and freshly ground black pepper to taste

▶ Serves six

Place a frying pan on medium heat. Add the whole spices to the pan and stir continuously until they are golden brown and releasing their aroma. Allow them to cool before grinding in an electric coffee grinder or pounding them in a mortar and pestle. Add the ground spices and chopped garlic to a stainless steel bowl. Add the yogourt and mix well. Pour some of this mixture into a ceramic baking dish. Lay the chicken breasts on top and cover with more marinating mixture. Refrigerate overnight.

Preheat an oven to 350°F/175°C. Set a vegetable steamer on medium heat. Set a frying pan on medium high heat.

Remove the chicken breasts from the refrigerator. Scrape excess marinade from the breasts. Season with salt. Add oil to the frying pan. Sear the chicken breasts to a golden brown on both sides. Transfer the breasts to a baking sheet and place them in the oven for 10 minutes to finish cooking.

Steam the fiddleheads for 10 minutes. When they are cooked, transfer them to a mixing bowl and toss with the butter and seasonings.

Presentation:
Warm six plates. Place a chicken breast in the center of each plate. Surround each breast with steamed fiddleheads. Serve at once.

Navarin of Lamb with Herb Butter

The preparation for this dish should be done three days before you plan to serve it. The lamb should marinate for two days and should be served the day after you cook it. The herb butter may be prepared weeks in advance if you wish. After it is used for this dish it may be used in other ways, like on grilled steaks or hamburgers.

FOR THE LAMB:

2 lbs./800 g lamb shoulder or leg

2 cups/480 mL Cabernet Sauvignon wine

1 Spanish onion, peeled and roughly chopped

1 carrot, peeled and roughly chopped

1 celery root, scrubbed and roughly chopped

3 cloves garlic, split in half

2 bay leaves

2 Tbsp./30 mL sunflower oil

1 cup/240 mL Tomato Sauce (page 156)

FOR THE HERB BUTTER:

2 Tbsp./30 mL shallots, cut into brunoise

12 cracked black peppercorns

1/2 cup/120 mL Cabernet Sauvignon wine

1 lb./455 g butter, at room temperature

Salt to taste

3 Tbsp./45 mL chopped parsley

1 Tbsp./15 mL roughly chopped rosemary

FOR THE GARNISH VEGETABLES:

1 cup/240 mL fresh green peas

18 small new potatoes, cooked and peeled

6 small carrots, peeled and cooked

1 cup/240 mL Lamb Jus (page 15)

▶Serves six

Cut the lamb into large bite-sized cubes. Place the cubes in a plastic storage container that has a lid. Add the rest of the ingredients for the lamb, except the oil and tomato sauce. Cover and marinate in the refrigerator for two days.

Place the shallots for the herb butter in a saucepan with the peppercorns and the wine. Simmer until the liquid has almost completely evaporated. Cut the butter into cubes and place them in the bowl of an electric mixer and beat. While the machine is running, add the wine mixture. Continue beating and add the salt and chopped herbs. Roll this mixture up using waxed paper to form two cylinders and store in the freezer.

Preheat an oven to 325°F/165°C. Heat a large saucepan or Dutch oven on medium heat. Sear the lamb pieces in the oil without stirring, for 4 minutes on each side. Add the vegetables from the marinade and gently sauté for 20 minutes until they are golden brown.

Add the tomato sauce and continue to cook until all the liquid has evaporated and the mixture is an even brown color. Add the wine from the marinade and bring to the boil. Skim any foam from the surface.

Add the lamb jus and return to the boil, then

reduce to a simmer. Season with salt and cover with a lid. Place in the oven to braise for 60 minutes. Strain the cooking liquid into a saucepan and continue to boil. Separate the vegetables from the meat and discard the vegetables. Return the meat to the cooking liquid. Keep warm.

Cook the garnish vegetables separately and keep them warm. Whisk cold herb butter into the simmering stew until all the butter has melted.

Presentation:

Warm six dinner plates. Place some lamb and sauce in the center of each plate. Arrange the garnish vegetables on top. Serve at once.

Lloyd Pope at Palmerston.

Nick Schaut at Palmerston.

Grilled New York Steak with Leek Vinaigrette
and Gaufrette Potatoes

T his recipe gives you a chance to explore the myriad uses of the mandolin. The mandolin originated in France where it is indispensable for producing perfect slices and julienne of vegetables. The gaufrette potato, or waffle, looks like a woven potato chip. Very impressive to look at, delicious to eat, and deceptively easy, albeit time consuming, to produce.

FOR THE POTATOES:

4 Yukon Gold potatoes

2 cups/480 mL sunflower oil

Salt to taste

FOR THE LEEKS:

3 leeks, split and washed

FOR THE VINAIGRETTE:

1 egg yolk

1 tsp./5 mL dry mustard powder

1 Tbsp./15 mL Dijon mustard

1 Tbsp./15 mL white wine vinegar

1 tsp./5 mL fresh lemon juice

2 Tbsp./30 mL sunflower oil

Salt and freshly ground black pepper to taste

FOR THE STEAK:

6, 6-oz./170-g New York steaks (see Note page 59)

Salt and freshly ground black pepper to taste

1 Tbsp./15 mL sunflower oil

▶ Serves six

Peel the potatoes. Pour the oil into a saucepan and bring the temperature to 300°F/150°C. Set the mandolin to the crinkle cut function with a $1/8$-inch/.3-cm width. Run a potato over the blade once, then turn the potato 90 degrees and run it over the blade again. A woven potato chip should fall from the apparatus. Usually adjustments have to be made in the width of the cut to get the waffled look in the chip just right. It should be thin enough to have tiny holes in it. Once you get the right adjustment, keep going with the cutting pattern. Cut the gaufrette potatoes only a few at a time. If you let them pile up before cooking they will oxidize and turn a horrible shade of grey. Cook the potatoes five or six at a time in the hot oil. Move the potatoes in

the oil so that they cook evenly. When they are golden brown all over, remove them with a slotted spoon to drain on paper towels. Salt them.

Place a pot of salted water on to boil. Cook the leeks in the boiling water for 5 minutes, or until they are tender, but not mushy. Remove them with a slotted spoon to drain on paper towels.

Remember, when making an emulsion, all your ingredients should be at room temperature. Place the egg yolk, both mustards, vinegar, and lemon juice in a stainless steel bowl. Whisk in the oil and season with salt and pepper. Pour the vinaigrette into a baking dish. Squeeze all the excess water from the leeks and press them into the vinaigrette, so that it has a chance to penetrate all the inner recesses of the leek. Reserve.

Prepare a gas or charcoal barbeque for cooking. Season the steaks and lightly oil them. Grill them according to your preference.

Garnish with a slice of Herb Butter (page 56) if you wish, after you turn the steaks.

Presentation:

Place a steak on each plate, accompanied by a leek in vinaigrette and a mound of gaufrette potatoes. Serve at once.

▶ ## Choosing steaks

Choose well-marbled dry-aged beef for your steaks. It is useful to know how long the beef has been aging. The optimum aging time is between two and four weeks. Smaller owner-operated butcher shops are usually the best places to go for well-aged beef.

Rob and Michael at Palmerston.

Trifle with Preserved Summer Fruits

Here's a way to present fruits from another season without resorting to purchasing the fruits out of season, when they are usually expensive and tasteless. If you have taken the time to preserve the fruits at their peak, then this recipe will yield delicious results.

1 recipe Génoise (page 21)
3 cups/720 mL Summer Fruits in Rum (page 111)
1 cup/240 mL 35% whipping cream

1 cup/240 mL Crème Anglaise (page 19)
3 Tbsp./45 mL kirsch

▶ Serves six

Preheat an oven to 350°F/175°C. Prepare the génoise batter according to the directions, but instead of baking the cake in a round spring-form cake pan, use a baking sheet lined with silicone or parchment paper. Bake until golden brown. Cool for 30 minutes before slicing the cake horizontally into as many slices as you can.

Whip the cream to stiff peaks. Fold in the crème anglaise. Place a thin layer of génoise in the bottom of a large glass bowl. Sprinkle with kirsch. Slice the fruit and spread it on the first layer of génoise. Cover with a layer of cream mixture.

Repeat this sequence of layering until the bowl is full. The last layer should be fruit. Chill for 2 hours before serving.

Presentation:

Scoop some trifle onto each plate and top with some syrup from the preserved fruit. Serve at once.

Baked Rhubarb Tart with Marzipan Sauce

FOR THE PASTRY:

1 lb./455 g Sweet Pastry (page 24)

FOR THE FILLING:

3 cups/720 mL rhubarb, cut into batons

1 cup/240 mL sugar

1/2 recipe Génoise (page 21)

FOR THE SAUCE:

1 cup/240 mL Crème Anglaise (page 19)

3 Tbsp./45 mL almond paste

1 Tbsp./15 mL kirsch

▶ Serves twelve

Preheat an oven to 350°F/175°C. Roll the pastry out to a thickness of 1/8 inch/.3 cm. Grease and dust with flour, a 10-inch/25-cm scalloped tart form with a removable base.

Roll the pastry up onto the rolling pin and drape it over the form, making sure to settle the pastry into every nook and cranny. Fill the tart form with baking beans and blind bake for 30 minutes or until golden brown. Cool for 15 minutes and remove the baking beans. Reserve.

Macerate the rhubarb batons with the sugar for 30 minutes. Meanwhile, prepare the génoise batter. Fill the tart form with two-thirds of the macerated rhubarb batons. Hold back one-third for the final layer. Place the macerating liquid in a saucepan on the stove and reduce it to a syrupy consistency. Pour the génoise batter into the tart shell with the rhubarb. Arrange the final layer of rhubarb atop the batter in a

decorative circular pattern. Bake for 35 minutes or until the rhubarb is tender and the génoise batter has set to a golden brown. Cool the baked tart for 20 minutes, then paint the surface of the tart with the reduced macerating liquid.

Warm the crème anglaise indirectly in a double boiler or over a saucepan of simmering water. In another bowl mix the almond paste with the kirsch.

Add 1 Tbsp./15 mL warm crème anglaise to the almond paste and mix it in thoroughly using a wooden spoon or your fingers. Keep adding crème anglaise gradually until the almond paste is completely dissolved in the crème anglaise.

Presentation:

Divide the tart into 12 equal slices. Pour some sauce onto each plate and top with a slice of tart. Serve at once.

It was in a café in Northern Germany that I first discovered how delicious marzipan could be. My friend and colleague Michael Stadtländer had brought me to Café Niederegger, in his hometown of Lübeck. The café fronted a large marzipan-producing business. The Lübecker marzipan torte that we ate with our delicious coffee was out of this world. The intensity and delicacy of the flavors and textures were woven together so brilliantly. It was a revelation.

Rhubarb Crisp with Vanilla Cream

Here is a simple spring dessert idea. It's delicious warm, crisp and straight from the oven with the cool cream flowing from the heat.

FOR THE RHUBARB CRISP:

3 cups/720 mL rhubarb, cut into batons

1 cup/240 mL sugar

$^1/_2$ cup/120 mL sifted pastry flour

$^1/_2$ cup/120 mL cubed butter

$^1/_2$ cup/120 mL brown sugar

$^1/_2$ cup/120 mL rolled oats

FOR THE VANILLA CREAM:

$^1/_2$ vanilla bean, split

2 Tbsp./30 mL sugar

1 cup/240 mL 35% whipping cream

▶Serves six

Preheat an oven to 350°F/175°C. Mix the rhubarb batons and sugar in a large mixing bowl. Grease a 9-inch/23-cm square glass baking dish. Mix the flour with the rhubarb. Transfer the rhubarb mixture to the baking dish and reserve. Cream the butter and brown sugar in another mixing bowl, then add the rolled oats. Mix well. Spread this mixture over the rhubarb and bake for 40 minutes or until the rhubarb is tender and the topping is golden brown. Cool for 10 minutes.

Scrape the gummy resin from the vanilla bean. Using your fingers, work the sugar and the vanilla resin together until you have a homogeneous mixture. Whisk the cream with the sugar and vanilla mixture until the cream thickens to soft peaks.

Presentation:

Scoop generous spoonfuls of crisp onto each plate. Spoon the cream on top. Serve at once.

Gooseberry Fool with Warm Hazelnut Pastry
and Blackberry Purée

FOR THE PASTRY:

2 cups/480 mL toasted, peeled, and crushed
  hazelnuts

1 lb./455 g Puff Pastry (page 23)

1/2 cup/120 mL large-grained sugar

FOR THE GOOSEBERRY FOOL:

2 cups/480 mL gooseberries, washed

1 cup/240 mL sugar

2 cups/480 mL 35% whipping cream

1 cup/240 mL Blackberry Purée (page 114)

▶Serves six

Preheat an oven to 350°F/175°C. Place the
hazelnuts on a baking sheet and bake them for
15 minutes or until they color slightly. While
they are still warm, gather them up in a tea
towel and rub the towel with the heel of your
hand. This will loosen the skins. Separate the
hazelnuts from their skins and gather them up
again in the tea towel. This time, crush the nuts
using a rolling pin.

Roll the puff pastry out to a thickness of
1/4 inch/.6 cm. Sprinkle the counter and the
pastry with the crushed nuts and the large-
grained sugar as you roll. The result will be
pastry that is imbedded with large-grained
sugar and crushed hazelnuts.

Once the pastry is rolled out, use a 4-inch/
10-cm round cutter to cut six rounds. Place the
rounds on a baking sheet and refrigerate.

Heat the gooseberries and the sugar in a
saucepan over low heat. Stir well and cover.
Simmer the gooseberries until they burst.
Transfer the cooked gooseberries to a food
processor and purée. Refrigerate for 30 minutes. Whip the cream to stiff peaks. Fold the
gooseberry purée into the whipped cream. Chill.

Bake the pastry rounds at 350°F/175°C for
20 minutes or until they are golden brown.

Presentation:

Place one round of warm pastry on each plate.
Place a large dollop of gooseberry fool on each
pastry. Drizzle blackberry purée over each
plate. Serve at once.

Maple Walnut Ice Cream in Maple Crisp
with Riesling Poached Pear

Not many people will actually go out and make maple syrup. I think it is one of those sweet condiments whose origin is often taken for granted. In fact, it is unique to North America and has a taste that is unique as well. It takes 40 gallons of sugar maple sap to produce 1 gallon of maple syrup. I use it as a regular sugar substitute in the crisps and the ice cream, with delicious results.

FOR THE MAPLE CRISPS:

1 recipe Vanilla Wafer Batter (page 25) (substitute granulated maple sugar for the sugar in the recipe)

FOR THE MAPLE WALNUT ICE CREAM:

1 recipe Crème Anglaise (page 19) (substitute maple syrup for the sugar)

1 cup/240 mL shelled walnuts

1 Tbsp./15 mL unsalted butter

Salt to taste

FOR THE RIESLING POACHED PEARS:

1, 25-oz./750-mL bottle Riesling wine

1 cup/240 mL sugar

1 vanilla bean, split and scraped

6 firm Bosc pears

▶ Serves six

Cut a maple leaf template for making the crisps. The template should be cut from a plastic yogourt or sour cream container lid, with a sharp craft knife.

Preheat an oven to 350°F/175°C. Grease a baking sheet with butter. Place the maple leaf template in one corner of the tray. Use a spatula to spread the maple wafer batter evenly inside the template. Repeat until there are at least six maple-leaf shaped wafers on the tray. Bake for 12 minutes or until golden brown. Remove the wafers and transfer each one into a bowl or deep saucer so the wafer's edges curl up slightly as it cools. Reserve.

Place the maple anglaise in an ice cream maker and process. Meanwhile, mix the walnuts with the butter and salt, and toast on a baking sheet for 6 minutes or until the walnuts color slightly. Cool in the refrigerator. After the ice cream is frozen, fold the toasted walnuts

into it. Return the ice cream to the freezer.

Place a large soup pot on the stove with the wine, sugar, and scraped vanilla bean. Peel the pears carefully, following the contours of the pear and not peeling away too much flesh. Use a melon baller to scoop the core from the bottom of the pear. As you peel and core the pears, place them immediately into the wine mixture to prevent oxidation. Poach the pears at a simmer, covered, for 60 minutes or until they are tender throughout, but not mushy.

Presentation:

Place a maple leaf wafer in the center of each plate. Slice the pears in half and then slice them thinly but not all the way through, so each pear half can be fanned. Place fanned halves on either side of the wafer. Place one scoop of ice cream in each wafer. Drizzle some pear poaching liquid on each fanned pear half. Serve at once.

Preserved Fruit Upside-Down Cake

1 cup/240 mL Plums in Vanilla Syrup, drained
(page 111)

1 cup/240 mL Apricots in Vanilla Syrup, drained
(page 111)

1 recipe Génoise (page 21)

▶ Serves twelve

Preheat an oven to 350°F/175°C. Use a
10-inch/25-cm springform cake pan to prepare
this recipe. Grease the bottom and sides of the
pan with butter and dust with flour. Arrange
a thick layer of apricots and plums in an
attractive circular pattern on the base of the
springform pan.

   Pour the cake batter over the fruit in
the springform pan. Bake for 35 minutes or
until the cake springs back to the touch or a

toothpick inserted in the cake comes out clean.
Cool the cake for 15 minutes before inverting
onto a cake plate. Meanwhile, pour 1 cup/
240 mL of the juice from the preserved fruits
into a saucepan. Boil until it thickens to a
syrup. Reserve.

Presentation:

Pour the syrup over the fruit. Cut a slice of
cake onto each plate. Serve at once.

*For this recipe you can
use any fruit that you
have preserved from last
summer, as long as it is not
puréed. Here, I use apricot
halves and plum halves.
Save the juice from the jars
to glaze the cake before
serving.*

Beet Pickled Wild Leeks

For about two weeks every spring, the forest floor is covered with wild leeks. Most years I am so excited about working with them in their fresh state that I forget about preserving them. This recipe uses only the bulbs because the greens do not hold up to brining. The beets provide an interesting color. Wait until the end of the season, when the bulbs are large, to preserve them.

8 cups/2 litres wild leek bulbs
3 cups/720 mL white wine vinegar
1 cup/240 mL Tomato Consommé (page 14)

2 raw beets
Salt to taste

▶ Serving size

Sterilize 4, 1-pint/500-mL preserving jars according to directions on package. After cleaning the wild leeks, pack them into the jars. Bring the white wine vinegar and the consommé to the boil in a stainless steel soup pot and season with salt. Peel the beets and cut them into pieces. Evenly distribute the pieces among the jars. Pour the boiling brine up to the neck of each jar. Place a seal and crown on each jar, and process the jars in boiling water for 15 to 20 minutes.

Rhubarb Compote

Rhubarb compote is a good thing to have around when you need to whip up a dessert quickly. Add whipped cream and you have rhubarb fool. Add some quartered strawberries and call it dessert.

8 cups/2 litres rhubarb, washed and cut into chunks

4 cups/950 mL sugar

▶ Serving size

Macerate the rhubarb and sugar together in a stainless steel bowl. Sterilize 4, 1-pint/500-mL jars according to directions on package. Place the macerated rhubarb in a stainless steel soup pot, bring to the boil, and simmer, covered, for 5 minutes or until the rhubarb begins to break down and fall apart. Transfer the cooked rhubarb to the jars. Place a seal and crown on each jar and process in boiling water for 15 minutes.

Summer

In the kitchen at Palmerston.

Vegetarian Ceviche on Potato Crisp

I *first discovered the piquant and refreshing simplicity of ceviche during a holiday in Mexico. I bought octopus ceviche on the beach from a wandering vendor. What could be more perfect on a hot summer day? It was satisfying but not heavy, with no heat required to cook it.*

Although ceviche is typically a technique to prepare fish, I offer this as a vegetarian dish.

2 medium-sized Yukon Gold potatoes

1 cup/240 mL sunflower oil

¼ English cucumber, washed and cut into brunoise

1 ripe tomato, washed and cut into brunoise

½ small red onion, cut into brunoise

3 Tbsp./45 mL sweet potato, peeled and cut into brunoise and blanched

1 Tbsp./15 mL roughly chopped fresh cilantro

Salt to taste

3 Tbsp./45 mL fresh lime juice

½ green chili, finely chopped

▶ Serves six

Peel and julienne the potatoes by hand or with a mandolin. Pour the oil into a stainless steel saucepan and heat to 250°F/120°C. Blanch the potato in small batches for 15 seconds. The object is to soften the potato, but not to cook it crisp. Next, shape the blanched potato into 12 little free-form nests.

Chop the remaining vegetables and combine with cilantro, salt, lime juice, and chili.

While the vegetables are marinating, increase the temperature of the oil to 350°F/175°C. Fry the potato nests until they are golden and crisp. Season with salt.

Presentation:

Mound some of the vegetable mixture on each potato nest and serve.

In the kitchen at Palmerston.

Curry and Yogourt Chicken Skewers

FOR THE MARINADE:

1 Tbsp./15 mL whole cumin seed

1 tsp./5 mL whole coriander seed

1/4 tsp./1.2 mL whole fenugreek

1/4 tsp./1.2 mL whole sweet cumin seed

1 small green chili, finely chopped

1/4 tsp./1.2 mL turmeric

1/2 clove garlic, finely chopped

1 Tbsp./15 mL fresh lime juice

1 cup/240 mL plain yogourt

FOR THE CHICKEN:

2 boneless skinless chicken breasts

12 bamboo skewers

Salt to taste

▶Serves six

Combine the whole spices in a frying pan and slowly toast them over low-medium heat, stirring constantly, until they turn golden and start to release their aroma. Remove the pan and cool to room temperature. Pulverize the seeds in a spice or coffee grinder and return them to a stainless steel mixing bowl. Add the chili, turmeric, garlic, and lime juice. Add the yogourt and mix well.

Cut the chicken into 12 equal pieces and pound each piece flat with the heel of a small saucepan or a meat pounder. Thread each piece onto a skewer and marinate the skewers in the refrigerator for up to 24 hours.

When you are ready to cook, remove the skewers from the marinade and scrape off any excess. Season with salt and either grill them on the barbecue or griddle them in the kitchen. In either case, they take approximately 2 minutes per side to cook.

Presentation:

Please the skewers all in a row on a platter with a nice sprig of fresh cilantro as a garnish.

Three Tapas
Clams with Paprika

1 Tbsp./15 mL fine olive oil

1 clove garlic, finely chopped

1 tsp./5 mL Spanish paprika

12 littleneck clams

2 Tbsp./30 mL fino sherry

Salt and freshly ground black pepper

1 tsp./5 mL sherry vinegar

1 Tbsp./15 mL chopped parsley

I've always felt an affinity to Spain—its culture and its people. I first visited Spain in 1977 to pay a surprise visit on an old friend. My intended one-week stay stretched to one month. I have been back several times since, and one thing I particularly enjoy is the tapas culture. You go out with friends on an ambulatory dinner quest, visiting several establishments for a small plate of the house specialty and a glass of chilled fino. It's a really fun way to dine.

▶Serves six

Heat the olive oil in a large saucepan and gently sauté the garlic. Add the paprika. Stir and then add the clams. Add the sherry and then close the lid and boil for 5 minutes or until the clam shells open by themselves. Remove the lid and let the clams cool in their shells. When they are cool enough to handle, separate the clams from the shells. Select 12 of the nicest half shells. Arrange these on a serving platter and place one clam in each shell. Taste the cooking liquid for salt and pepper and add sherry vinegar.

Presentation:

Spoon a little of the cooking liquid into each clam shell. Sprinkle with parsley and serve.

Toasted Almonds

1 lb./455 g whole almonds

2 Tbsp./30 mL fine olive oil

Sea salt to taste

▶ Serves six

Preheat an oven to 350°F/175°C. Bring a big pot of water to the boil and add the almonds. After 5 minutes, drain them and pop them out of their skins as they cool. Spread the skinless almonds on a baking sheet. Coat them with the olive oil and roast them in the oven, stirring occasionally, for 10 minutes, or until they are golden brown. They burn quite easily once they are past this stage, so be careful. Remove the almonds and sprinkle them with salt.

Presentation:

When the almonds have cooled to room temperature, transfer them to a bowl and serve.

Roasted Peppers with Garlic and Oregano

1, 1 pint/500-mL jar Roasted Red Peppers (page 155)

1 clove garlic, finely chopped

2 Tbsp./30 mL olive oil for cooking

$^1/_2$ tsp./2.5 mL chopped fresh oregano

1 tsp./5 mL sherry vinegar

Salt and freshly ground black pepper to taste

▶ Serves six

Cut the peppers into wide strips. Gently sauté the garlic in olive oil, add the peppers, and continue to sauté for 5 minutes. Stir in the oregano and finish with sherry vinegar. Season with salt and black pepper. Cool to room temperature.

Presentation:

Fold the strips of peppers in half and skewer with a toothpick. Arrange them on a platter and serve.

Lemongrass Shrimp

The lemongrass in this recipe takes the place of a skewer. But if you can't find lemongrass, or don't feel like carving little lemongrass spears, you could always substitute regular bamboo skewers. However, the subtle flavor that the lemongrass infuses into this dish makes the carving exercise well worth the effort.

FOR THE SHRIMP:

6 lemongrass shoots

12 large shrimp, peeled and deveined

FOR THE COCKTAIL SAUCE:

1/4 cup/60 mL oven-dried tomato purée (see below) or ketchup

1/2 cup/120 mL Mayonnaise (page 18)

2 tsp./10 mL cognac

Salt to taste

FOR THE COURT BOUILLON:

4 1/4 cups/1 litre water

1/3 cup/80 mL white wine vinegar

1 Spanish onion, sliced

1 carrot, peeled and sliced on the bias

1 celery root, peeled and sliced on the bias

1 leek, split, washed, and sliced on the bias

1 fennel bulb, washed and sliced lengthwise

1 bay leaf

15 black peppercorns, coarsely ground

Salt to taste

▶ Serves six

Split the lemongrass spears in half lengthwise. Carve and sharpen the root end into a point. Insert the spear into the shrimp, making sure the shrimp is firmly secured. When you are finished, the shrimp should be straight, instead of curved as a shrimp naturally appears. Skewer two shrimp on each lemongrass shoot.

Preheat an oven to 275°F/135°C. To oven-dry tomatoes, simply quarter and seed two medium beefsteak tomatoes and roast them in the oven until they are shrivelled but not caramelized. Purée the tomatoes in a blender, then mix the purée, or ketchup, with the mayonnaise and cognac. Add salt.

Bring the water and the vinegar to the boil and add the sliced vegetables. Add the spices and salt. Simmer for 10 minutes. Add the shrimp and continue to simmer until the shrimp appear opaque, about 2 minutes. Be careful not to overcook.

Presentation:

Transfer shrimp from the court bouillon to a serving platter. Place a small dish of cocktail sauce in the center of the platter. Garnish the platter with vegetables from the court bouillon. Serve at once.

Poached Eggs with Bacon Rösti
and Organic Tomatoes

FOR THE RÖSTI:

8-oz./225-g piece smoked side bacon

2 shallots, peeled and cut into brunoise

6 medium Yukon Gold potatoes

6 Tbsp./90 mL unsalted butter

Salt to taste

FOR THE TOMATOES:

6 ripe organic tomatoes, washed

Salt and freshly ground black pepper to taste

FOR THE EGGS:

8 cups/2 litres water

2 Tbsp./30 mL white wine vinegar

12 eggs, at room temperature

▶Serves six

Cut the bacon into lardons. Sauté gently for 5 minutes. This process will render fat and crisp the bacon. Add the shallot when the bacon is almost crisp. Continue to sauté for 2 minutes. Drain the fat from the bacon-shallot mixture. Reserve.

Peel the potatoes. Heat an 8-inch/20 cm nonstick frying pan and add 1 Tbsp./15 mL butter. While the butter is melting, grate one potato. Pick up the gratings and squeeze out all the excess water. (You will be surprised by how much there is.) Distribute the potatoes evenly over the entire surface of the pan. Add $\frac{1}{6}$ of the bacon mixture and distribute that evenly as well. Fry for 5 minutes, or until golden and crispy, then flip. Fry for another 5 minutes and transfer to a baking sheet. Repeat this process five times until you have six rösti on a baking sheet. Reserve.

Slice each tomato thickly and arrange the slices on a tray. Season with salt and freshly ground black pepper. Reserve.

Bring the poaching water to a boil and add the vinegar. Reduce to simmer and gently break the eggs into the water. You may have to regulate the temperature to keep the water at the simmering point. Poach eggs to desired doneness.

Presentation:

Warm six plates. Warm the rösti in the oven. Place one rösti on each plate. Arrange sliced tomatoes in a circular pattern on each rösti. Using a slotted spoon, carefully remove each egg from the poaching water. Place two eggs on each arrangement of tomatoes and serve right away.

Chanterelle Strudel

Chanterelles grow wild everywhere in Canada. Look for mushrooms that are small and dry, as opposed to exploded-looking and wet. In recent years they have become more popular in cooking so there are many more people foraging for them. Until you can learn to identify these little gems on your own it is advisable to purchase them from an experienced forager.

FOR THE PASTRY:
1 1/2 cups/360 mL bread flour
3/4 cup/180 mL cold water
3 Tbsp./45 mL melted butter
pinch salt
2 tsp./10 mL fresh lemon juice

FOR THE FILLING:
1/4 loaf white bread, cut into cubes
1/2 cup/120 mL milk
2 slices smoked bacon

1 small onion, cut into brunoise
2 oz./56 g unsalted butter
1 lb./454 g fresh chanterelles
1 egg
1 Tbsp./15 mL chopped parsley
1 tsp./5 mL chopped fresh thyme
Salt and freshly ground black pepper to taste

FOR PULLING THE STRUDEL:
1/4 cup/60 mL melted butter

▶ Serves six

Combine the ingredients for the pastry in a stainless steel bowl. Take this loose mixture, invert it onto a smooth surface, and knead vigorously for 10 minutes. Form the dough into a ball and cover it with plastic wrap. Let the dough rest for 4 hours at room temperature. This will give you plenty of time to prepare the filling.

Soak the bread cubes in the milk for 5 minutes. Squeeze out the cubes and discard excess milk. Return the bread to the working bowl.

Dice the bacon and gently sauté with the onion and butter for 5 minutes.

Brush the chanterelles and split them if they are too large. Add the chanterelles to the bacon and onion mixture and continue to sauté for

5 more minutes. Add the bacon mixture to the bread cubes with the egg, parsley, and thyme. Mix well by hand to make sure that the bread mixture is evenly distributed. Adjust seasoning.

Now, if 4 hours have elapsed, you may begin to pull the strudel dough. A card table is a good work surface for this step. Drape it with a smooth tablecloth. Preheat an oven to 350°F/ 175°C. Melt the butter and keep it and a pastry brush on hand. Dust the tablecloth with flour. Place the dough in the center. Roll the dough out into a round as you would for a pie crust, as thinly as you can. Start to stretch and pull the dough by lifting from underneath using your fingertips, but not fingernails, and drawing it towards you as if you were beckoning it. The object is to cover the card table completely with dough and drape it over the sides as though it were a tablecloth so thin you could read a newspaper through it. It takes lots of practice, and don't be discouraged if you tear the dough—simply pinch it back together.

Once the dough covers the table, paint the surface of the dough with the melted butter. Place the bacon filling along one edge of the dough to a height of approximately 1½ inches/ 3.8 cm. Draw the dough over the mushroom filling along the whole length of the table. Gently begin rolling the dough. Stop periodically to check your work and to straighten the roll to make sure it is tight. Make sure that you finish the roll with the dough forming a seam on the bottom of the strudel. Cut the strudel in half with a sharp knife and transfer each half to a nonstick baking tray. Bake on the upper shelf of the oven for 30 minutes or until golden brown.

Presentation:

When the strudel is still warm, but cool enough to eat, slice it into ½-inch/12-mm pieces and place them on a serving platter. Serve at once.

"Coup de Feu" Palmerston.

Rob McDonald "tete a tete" with Julia.

Mediterranean Salad with Olive Toasts

This is a cooked salad presented at room temperature. The use of garlic, olives, and saffron typify the Mediterranean region. Beware if the saffron you are purchasing seems inexpensive; use genuine saffron for this recipe.

FOR THE SALAD:

1 1/2 Tbsp./22.5 mL white wine vinegar

1/4 tsp./1.2 mL genuine saffron

4 Tbsp./60 mL olive oil for cooking

1/2 lb./225 g button mushrooms, quartered

3 carrots, peeled and cut into batons

3 celery stalks, washed and cut into batons

1/4 lb./113 g whole Niçoise olives

1 head of broccoli, washed and broken into florets

1/2 head of cauliflower, washed and broken into florets

1 clove garlic, finely chopped

Salt and freshly ground black pepper to taste

2 tomatoes, cut into large concassé

FOR THE TOASTS:

6 slices of bread, crusts removed, quartered, and lightly toasted

1/4 lb./113 g Niçoise olives, pitted

▶ Serves six

Heat the vinegar and saffron in a small saucepan over medium heat. The idea is to infuse the saffron into the vinegar, not unlike steeping a cup of tea. The result should be an intensely colored orangey-red clear liquid that you will use later to color and flavor the salad.

Pour the olive oil into a large frying pan and heat to just below smoking point. Stir in the mushrooms, carrots, celery, olives, broccoli, and cauliflower. Add the garlic, then season with salt and pepper. On high heat, add the saffron infusion and cover. Steam for 1 minute and remove the lid.

Stir in the tomatoes and then allow to cool to room temperature.

Next, purée the olives for the toast and spread each toast quarter with olive paste.

Presentation:

Spoon some salad onto each of six plates and garnish with four of the olive toasts.

Ceviche Salad with Avocado

3 avocadoes, firm but ripe

1 Tbsp./15 mL lime juice

$^1/_4$ lb./113 g white shrimp, peeled, deveined and chopped

$^1/_4$ lb./113 g scallops, diced

1 Tbsp./15 mL diced red onion

1 Tbsp./15 mL diced tomato

1 Tbsp./15 mL diced cucumber

1 small green chili, finely diced

1 Tbsp./15 mL roughly chopped fresh cilantro

6 small sprigs of fresh cilantro

Salt to taste

▶Serves six

Split the avocadoes in half lengthwise. Scoop out bite-sized pieces of avocado from each half and reserve the shells. Mix the lime juice, shrimp, and scallops in a bowl. After 15 minutes, add the remaining vegetables and chili. Gently combine with the avocado pieces, cilantro, and salt.

Presentation:

Fill each avocado shell with the ceviche mixture. Garnish with a cilantro leaf and serve on small salad plates.

Steamed Beets with Mustard Dressing

I use a variety of organic beets for this recipe. The different vibrant colors really make this dish gorgeous. However, if you do not have access to candycane or golden beets, choose small, red beets with their greens attached.

FOR THE DRESSING:

1 Tbsp./15 mL dry mustard powder

1 Tbsp./15 mL white wine vinegar

1 Tbsp./15 mL honey

1 egg yolk

1 Tbsp./15 mL fresh lemon juice

3 Tbsp./45 mL sunflower oil

Salt and freshly ground black pepper to taste

FOR THE BEETS:

6 small golden beets

6 small candycane beets

6 small red beets

Small piece of peeled horseradish root

▶Serves six

Use a blender or food processor for the dressing. Dissolve the dry mustard in the vinegar and pour into the blender. Add the honey, egg yolk, and lemon juice. While the machine is running add the oil in a slow, steady stream. You must do this slowly for successful emulsification of the egg yolk/vinegar mixture with the oil. If you add the oil too quickly, the finished dressing may have a curdled appearance. Add salt and pepper to taste. Transfer the dressing to a storage jar.

Meanwhile, wash and trim the beets, reserving the greens separately. Cook the different beets in separate pots in plenty of salted water. Cooking the different beets in separate pots prevents the colors from bleeding. Boil briskly for 30 minutes, or until the skins slide off easily with some thumb pressure. It is very important to thoroughly cook the beets.

Drain the cooked beets and, when they are cool enough to handle, peel the skins off. Slice each beet into discs.

Steam the beet tops for 2 minutes, cool, and chop roughly.

Presentation:

Pool some of the mustard dressing on each of six salad plates. Next, place a mound of the beet tops in the center of each pool of dressing. Place overlapping discs of the beets in a circular pattern directly on the greens. Garnish with a random grating of fresh horseradish and serve at room temperature.

Summer Salad with Crottin Chauvignol

3 individual crottin chauvignol cheeses
1 small head Boston lettuce
1 small head oak leaf lettuce
2 Tbsp./30 mL sunflower oil

2 Tbsp./30 mL walnut oil
1 Tbsp./15 mL white wine vinegar
Salt and freshly ground black pepper to taste
$1/8$ cup/30 mL freshly shelled walnuts

▶ Serves six

Preheat an oven to 250°F/120°C. Split the cheeses in half lengthwise and place them on a tray. Tear the lettuces up into a basin of cool water. Repeat with fresh water if necessary and dry in a salad spinner. Heat the cheese in the oven for 5 minutes, or until warmed but not melted.

Toss the salad greens with the oils and vinegar and seasonings.

Presentation:

Arrange the salad on six plates. Sprinkle walnut pieces over each plate. Using a spatula, transfer one piece of cheese onto the center of each plate and serve.

Sometimes the dishes I love are developed simply to capture the spirit of the wine they are to be served with. This salad is a good example. Crottin chauvignol is a small artisanal goat cheese made in the Loire district of France. It is widely known that the cheese is a perfect match with Sancerre, a wine that is also from the Loire Valley. However, since goat cheese and Sauvignon Blanc are a lovely match, one could substitute Sauvignon from anywhere with goat cheese from anywhere.

Eggplant Vinaigrette with Grilled Squid

This is a nice patio dish. You may prepare the eggplant the day before and the grilled squid may be added just before serving. I specify Sicilian eggplant for this recipe because I find it has a sweeter taste and a softer "eggy" texture. However, regular eggplant may be substituted with great results.

FOR THE MARINADE:

2 Tbsp./30 mL white wine vinegar

1 clove garlic, finely chopped

1 Tbsp./15 mL shallot, peeled and cut into brunoise

1 tsp./5 mL roughly chopped fresh oregano

Salt and freshly ground black pepper to taste

FOR THE EGGPLANT:

1 medium eggplant, washed (preferably Sicilian)

Salt to taste

4 Tbsp./60 mL olive oil for cooking

FOR THE SQUID:

3 squid, fresh or frozen

Salt and freshly ground black pepper to taste

1 Tbsp./15 mL fine olive oil

1 sweet red pepper, washed

▶Serves six

Combine the marinade ingredients. Slice the eggplant into rounds ³⁄₄-inch/1.9-cm thick. Season the rounds with salt and fry them in the olive oil, piece by piece, until each slice is golden brown on both sides. While they are still warm, transfer the slices to the marinade.

Meanwhile, prepare your barbeque for grilling. Slice the squid into rings but don't cut all the way through, so that the body is still in one piece resembling a comb. Mix the salt and pepper and olive oil together in a large bowl. Toss with the squid.

When the coals are hot, grill the squid and the red pepper. Toss the cooked squid in the marinade with the eggplant. Slice the charred red pepper into strips.

Presentation:

Arrange two slices of eggplant on each of six plates. Place a piece of squid on each eggplant. Garnish with strips of red pepper. Serve.

Facing page: Poached Eggs with Bacon Rösti and Organic Tomatoes (page 73)

Following page: Goat Cheese Tartlet with Flavored Oils (page 83)

French Fried Potatoes
with Lemon and Mayonnaise

FOR THE POTATOES:

6 medium Yukon Gold potatoes

8$^1/_2$ cups/2 litres sunflower oil

1 Tbsp./15 mL coarsely chopped fresh thyme

1 lemon, cut into 6 wedges

Salt to taste

FOR THE MAYONNAISE:

6 Tbsp./90 mL Mayonnaise (page 18)

▶ Serves six

Peel the potatoes and cut them into evenly-sized sticks at whatever thickness you prefer. Meanwhile, heat the oil in a large pot to 250°F/120°C. Blanch the potatoes in the oil until they are cooked but not yet turning golden. Remove them with a slotted spoon or skimmer and spread them out on a baking sheet to cool.

Increase the temperature of the oil to 350°F/175°C. Fry the potatoes in the oil until they are golden brown. Transfer them from the oil to a stainless steel bowl. Toss with thyme and salt. Serve at once with mayonnaise and lemon wedges.

*L*et's face it. People love fries. It intrigued me when I read that 70% of the fast food dollar is spent on potatoes in one form or another. I have always loved french fries and have been disappointed on numerous occasions over the years by poorly executed pommes frites. I use paper cones to serve my french fries which is how they are served in Belgium, where the pommes frites are second to none.

Facing page: Vanilla and Raspberry Sandwich
  (page 100)
Previous page: Mixed Tomato Salad with Fried Celery
  Root (page 86)

Rösti with Salmon Roe and Crème Fraîche

Prepare the Crème Fraîche a day ahead.

FOR THE RÖSTI:

6 medium Yukon Gold potatoes

3 Tbsp./45 mL unsalted butter

Salt to taste

▶Serves six

Preheat an oven to 250°F/120°C. Prepare six rösti as on page 73, omitting the bacon and shallots. Transfer them to a baking sheet and keep them warm in the oven.

FOR THE FILLING:

6 Tbsp./90 mL radish seedlings

3 Tbsp./45 mL Crème Fraîche (page 19)

6 Tbsp./90 mL salmon roe

Presentation:

Place ⅙ of each of the filling ingredients on the rösti, beginning with the radish seedlings and ending with the salmon roe. Repeat with the remaining rösti. Gently fold the rösti and place on each of six plates. Serve at once.

Roberta Belfry at Palmerston.

Palmerston kitchen from a dining perspective.

Goat Cheese Tartlet with Flavored Oils

FOR THE PASTRY:
1 lb./455 g Pie Pastry (page 24)

FOR THE FLAVORED OILS:
1/4 cup/60 mL Roasted Red Peppers (page 155)
1/4 cup/60 mL fine olive oil
1/4 cup/60 mL pitted Niçoise olives

FOR THE FILLING:
1 cup/240 mL milk

2 eggs
Pinch of freshly grated nutmeg
Salt and freshly ground black pepper to taste
3/4 cup/180 mL crumbled fresh goat cheese
6 Tbsp./90 mL Roasted Red Pepper strips (page 155)
1 bunch green onions, washed and sliced on the bias
6 cloves baked garlic
3 Tbsp./45 mL pitted Niçoise olives
1 tsp./5 mL dried rosemary

▶Serves six

Preheat an oven to 350°F/175°C. You will need individual 4-inch/10-cm scalloped tart forms to make this recipe. Butter and flour each form. Roll out the pastry to a thickness of 1/8 inch/ .3 cm and cut out 6, 7-inch/18-cm rounds. Drape each tart form with a round and make sure the pastry lines the form completely. Fill each form with baking beans (available at kitchen supply stores). Rest the forms in the refrigerator for 1 hour, then blind bake for 20 minutes or until pastry is golden brown.

Meanwhile, prepare the flavored oils. You will need a food processor and two squeeze bottles. Purée the roasted red peppers with half the olive oil. Pour the mixture into one of the squeeze bottles. Repeat the process with the olives and the remaining oil. Reserve.

Mix the milk, eggs, and spices vigorously in a stainless steel bowl. Evenly distribute the remaining ingredients in each of the six pre-baked tart forms. Fill each form just shy of the brim with the egg mixture and bake for 20 minutes or until the filling is golden brown and set.

Presentation:
Make a random squiggly pattern on six dinner plates with the oils from each of the squeeze bottles. Place a warm tart on each plate. Serve at once.

Chanterelle Toast with Red Wine Glaze

6 slices whole wheat bread, crusts removed

FOR THE GLAZE:

1 cup/240 mL dry red wine

1 Tbsp./15 mL cold butter, cut into small cubes

FOR THE CHANTERELLES:

2 Tbsp./30 mL butter

1 Tbsp./15 mL onion, cut into brunoise

1 Tbsp./15 mL finely minced smoked bacon

12 oz./342 g fresh chanterelles (see page 74)

1 Tbsp./15 mL roughly chopped Italian parsley

$^1/_2$ tsp./2.5 mL roughly chopped fresh thyme

Salt to taste

▶Serves six

Preheat an oven to 250°F/120°C and toast the crustless slices of bread. This will take approximately 30 minutes.

In the meantime, start to make the glaze. Bring the red wine to a boil in a stainless steel saucepan. Lower heat to simmer and reduce the wine to a syrupy consistency. While the wine is simmering, brush any debris from the chanterelles using a mushroom brush or a pastry brush. Heat the butter, onion, and bacon in a frying pan over medium high heat. Add the chanterelles and sauté for 5 minutes or until the mushrooms soften and begin to release liquid. Season with parsley, thyme, and salt.

Reduce the heat and keep the mushrooms warm.

Check on the toasts in the oven. They should be bone dry and slightly golden.

When the red wine has reached the syrup consistency, whisk in the small pieces of butter. Remove from the heat and reserve.

Presentation:

Place a toast in the center of each of six plates. Spoon $^1/_6$ of the chanterelle mixture on each toast. Spoon a small pool of glaze on either side of each toast. Serve at once.

Sausages with Sautéed Potatoes
and Tomato Sauce

FOR THE SAUSAGE MIX:

1 1/4 lbs./565 g ground pork neck

2 cloves garlic, finely diced

1/2 cup/120 mL sliced Roasted Red Peppers
(page 155)

1 tsp./5 mL finely chopped chili pepper

1 bay leaf, finely chopped

1/4 tsp./1.2 mL freshly ground nutmeg

1/2 tsp./2.5 mL roughly chopped summer savory

Salt to taste

Optional: lamb casings for sausage extruding machine

FOR THE POTATOES:

12 new potatoes

4 Tbsp./60 mL unsalted butter

Salt to taste

FOR THE SAUCE:

4 1/4 cups/1 litre Tomato Sauce (page 156)

2 Tbsp./30 mL fine olive oil

Salt and freshly ground black pepper to taste

▶ Serves six

Prepare all the seasonings and add them to the ground pork in a stainless steel bowl. Mix thoroughly by hand. Make a small patty and fry it on both sides. Taste this patty and adjust for seasonings.

If you are using a sausage machine, fill the cannister with your sausage mix, making sure there are no air pockets. Soak the casings in warm water to remove their salt and fit a length onto the end of the extruding nozzle. Fill the casings slowly. Make links and cut.

If you do not have access to a machine, form cylinders by hand. Fry the sausages in a cast iron frying pan with a tiny bit of oil, 4 minutes per side.

Cook the potatoes in boiling salted water and peel them while they are still warm. Slice them into discs and sauté gently in butter until golden brown on both sides.

Bring the tomato sauce to a boil. Simmer and reduce by one-third. Stir in the olive oil and adjust salt and freshly ground black pepper.

Presentation:

Place fried potatoes in a heap at one side of each of six plates. Place a sausage next to the potatoes. Pour some of the sauce onto the plate next to the sausage. Serve with mustard.

The art of sausage making has long been part of the culinary tradition of many countries. In Europe pork is the meat most commonly used. Charcuterie, or the art of making prepared pork dishes in France, is as varied as the number of villages there are in the country. Sausage making, hams, patés, and terrines all fall under the category of charcuterie. Sausages are traditionally presented in the intestines of the animal. This requires a special apparatus designed specifically for this purpose. If you do not have access to one, then this recipe may be prepared by shaping the patty into a sausage link. For best results, when you purchase the pork from the butcher ask that the total weight be approximately 30% fat.

Mixed Tomato Salad with Fried Celery Root
and Arugula

FOR THE DRESSING:

2 egg yolks

1 Tbsp./15 mL fresh lemon juice

1 tsp./5 mL white wine vinegar

1 tsp./5 mL Dijon mustard

2 Tbsp./30 mL fresh basil leaves

5 Tbsp./75 mL sunflower oil

2 Tbsp./30 mL 35% whipping cream

Salt and freshly ground black pepper to taste

FOR THE CELERY ROOT:

1/2 cup/120 mL julienne of celery root

1 cup/240 mL sunflower oil

Salt to taste

FOR THE TOMATOES:

2 red beefsteak tomatoes

2 yellow tomatoes

2 ripe green tomatoes

12 cherry tomatoes

12 arugula leaves

Salt and freshly ground black pepper to taste

▶ Serves six

Use a food processor to make the dressing. Process the egg yolks, lemon juice, vinegar, and mustard. Add the basil leaves and continue processing. Slowly add the sunflower oil. Season with salt and pepper. Trickle in the cream. Set aside the dressing.

Heat the oil for the celery root to 325°F/165°C in a small saucepan. Fry the celery root until crispy and golden. Remove from the oil with a slotted spoon. Season with salt. Reserve on a piece of paper towel.

Wash the tomatoes and slice into thick rounds. Season with salt and pepper and place on a tray.

Presentation:

Pour a little pool of dressing on each of six plates. Arrange the tomato slices in a pleasing pattern. Sprinkle with fried celery root. Garnish each plate with 2 leaves of arugula. Serve.

Summer Bean Risotto

2 cups/480 mL Tomato Consommé (page 14)

1 cup/240 mL Tomato Sauce (page 156)

$^1/_2$ cup/120 mL fresh, shucked fava beans

$^1/_2$ cup/120 mL fresh, shucked romano beans

$^1/_2$ cup/120 mL green beans

2 cloves garlic, halved

1 Tbsp./15 mL olive oil for cooking

1 cup/240 mL Italian short grain rice

2 shallots, peeled, cut into brunoise

2 Tbsp./30 mL dry white wine

2 Tbsp./30 mL 35% whipping cream

1 tsp./5 mL roughly chopped summer savory

$^1/_4$ cup/60 mL grated Parmigiano Reggiano

Salt and freshly ground black pepper to taste

2 Tbsp./30 mL fine olive oil

▶ Serves six

Heat the tomato consommé to a simmer in a saucepan.

Heat the tomato sauce in a separate pan and reduce the volume by one-third.

Soak the shucked beans in water to remove any grit. Cook them in boiling unsalted water until they are tender. Drain and reserve the beans.

Top the green beans and blanch them in salted water. Transfer the blanched green beans to a tray to cool. Slice them on the bias and reserve.

Gently sauté the garlic in the olive oil in a large saucepan for 2 minutes. Add the raw rice to the garlic and oil and stir over medium heat until the rice grains start to take on some golden color. Add the shallots to the rice. Reduce heat to simmer, and begin ladling the hot tomato consommé over the rice, one ladle at a time. Stir constantly while you are doing this because stirring helps to release starch into the mixture.

Add more consommé when the liquid is absorbed. When you have added approximately three-quarters of the tomato consommé, add the beans, one variety at a time, finishing with the green beans. Add the white wine and stir. Add the cream and the summer savory and stir. Add the grated cheese and stir very well.

Once the tomato sauce has reduced by one-third, add the fine olive oil and adjust seasoning.

Presentation:

Warm six plates. Place a mound of risotto in the center of each plate. Spoon a small pool of sauce on either side of the mound of risotto. Serve at once.

Lobster Bisque

FOR THE BISQUE:

3, 1-lb./454-g live lobsters

$^1/_4$ cup/60 mL olive oil for cooking

3 cloves garlic, roughly chopped

1 tsp./5 mL whole caraway seeds

1 Spanish onion, roughly chopped

$^1/_2$ fennel bulb, cleaned and roughly chopped

1 cup/240 mL Tomato Sauce (page 156)

3 cups/720 mL Chicken Stock (page 14)

FOR THE GARNISH:

2 Tbsp./30 mL finely chopped chives

▶Serves six

Bring a large stockpot three-quarters filled with salted water to a rolling boil. Plunge the lobsters in, one at a time, for 5 minutes each. Let them cool on the counter. Remove the claws and the tail section from the main body of the lobster. Cut the main body in half lengthwise. This operation will reveal the stomach of the lobster, which is near the head. Remove the stomach from each lobster and discard. Do your best to remove the claw meat and tail meat intact from their spiny shells. Reserve in the refrigerator.

Heat a large saucepan; add the oil and garlic. Stir for 1 minute, then add the caraway seed and the rest of the vegetables. Chop the lobster shells and add them to the vegetable mixture. Add the tomato sauce and continue to stir until almost all the liquid has evaporated and the tomato has changed to a rich, almost brown color. Add the chicken stock. Bring to a boil and cook for 10 minutes at simmering point. Strain the liquid from the shells, reserving the liquid.

Pound the shells will a mortar and pestle or pass them through a food mill. Mix the pounded shells with the cooking liquid and bring back to the boil. Pass through a medium strainer, allowing as much mashed shell and vegetable matter into the strained mixture as possible. Place the bisque back on the stove and reduce slowly by half.

Preheat an oven to 275°F/135°C. While the bisque is reducing, slice the tail meat into medallions and place in an ovenproof dish with the claw meat. Cover with foil and heat in the oven for 5 minutes.

Presentation:

Warm six large soup bowls. Place an equal amount of claw and tail meat in each bowl. Ladle some bisque into each bowl and garnish with finely chopped chives. Serve at once.

Sour Cherry Consommé

FOR THE SOUP:

5 lbs./2.25 kg fresh sour cherries

1, 25-oz./750-mL bottle Off Dry Riesling wine

1 1/2 cups/360 mL sugar

FOR THE GARNISH:

12 whole almonds

6 couplets of fresh sour cherries

▶ Serves six

Wash the sour cherries in cold water. Drain, and remove the stems. Transfer the cherries to a stainless steel saucepan. Add the wine and the sugar and bring to a boil. Reduce the heat to simmer, cover and cook for 15 minutes. Line a colander with three layers of cheesecloth. Position the colander over a stainless steel or glass bowl to catch the drips.

Transfer the sour cherries, liquid and all, to the cheesecloth. Fold the cheesecloth up and over the cherries. Place a weight on the cloth to gently press the cherry mash. (Gently is the key here because the gentler the press, the clearer the resulting liquid.) If you can fit this straining apparatus into your refrigerator, it is best to refrigerate the colander of cherries in the bowl overnight. The next day the resulting liquid should be clear and a brilliant shade of red. The taste should be just sweet enough to counter the extreme tartness of the sour cherries.

Blanch the almonds in boiling water for 5 minutes. Drain the water. While they are still warm, slip off their skins. Slice the almonds as thinly as you can.

Presentation:

Chill six clear glass soup bowls. Place some almonds in the base of each bowl. Ladle the soup into the bowls. Suspend a couplet of cherries over each rim. Serve at once.

Essence of Wild Mushroom
with Seared Shiitake Julienne

FOR THE SOUP:

1/2 cup/120 mL dried porcini mushrooms

1/4 lb./113 g oyster mushrooms

1/4 lb./113 g shiitake mushroom stems (save caps for garnish)

2 cloves garlic, halved

1 medium-sized Spanish onion

2 celery stalks, washed

4 egg whites

1 small bunch of fresh thyme

1 bay leaf

Salt and freshly ground black pepper to taste

8 cups/2 litres Tomato Consommé (page 14)

FOR THE GARNISH:

1/4 lb./113 g shiitake mushroom caps

1/4 lb./113 g ripe tomato, washed

▶Serves six

Cut all the mushrooms and vegetables for the soup into a rough dice. Make a clarification by combining these ingredients thoroughly with the egg whites in a stainless steel bowl. Season with the thyme, bay leaf, and black pepper, but do not add salt yet. Transfer the vegetables to a large stainless steel stockpot. Add the tomato consommé and slowly bring to the simmering point, stirring often. It is important to keep the ingredients suspended in the liquid while it is heating. The egg whites are slowly coagulating in response to the increased temperature. This coagulation is what will eventually clarify the soup.

Once the soup has reached the simmering point, a raft of ingredients should be forming on the surface. Once this raft has formed it is important not to disturb it. So, no more stirring.

Instead, you may reduce the temperature so that it is just under the simmering point and cover the pot. After 30 minutes, strain the soup through a colander lined with cheesecloth. It should be crystal clear.

Sear the shiitake stems in a hot frying pan with no oil until they are crispy and golden on both sides. This will take 5 minutes of close monitoring. Cut the tomato into quarters lengthwise and remove the seeds and membrane. Cut the trimmed quarters into brunoise. Cut the seared shiitake caps into julienne.

Presentation:

Heat six bowls. Divide the shiitake and the tomato among the bowls. Ladle mushroom essence into the bowls. Serve at once.

Seared Tuna
with Beet and Horseradish Beurre Blanc

6 Rösti (page 73)

$^1/_3$ cup/80 mL white wine vinegar

3 Tbsp./45 mL shallot, peeled and cut into brunoise

$^1/_3$ cup/80 mL dry white wine

1 tsp./5 mL cracked black peppercorns

6 small carrots, peeled

6 small beets

6 small bunches watercress

6, 4-oz./113-g fillets fresh tuna, at room temperature

Salt and freshly ground black pepper to taste

2 Tbsp./30 mL sunflower oil

2 Tbsp./30 mL cold butter, cut into small cubes

$^1/_4$ small beet, washed

2 Tbsp./30 mL grated fresh horseradish

▶Serves six

Make the rösti and reserve them on a baking sheet not touching each other.

Reduce the vinegar, shallots, white wine, and peppercorns in a small stainless steel pan until the reduction has reached a syrupy stage. Remove from the heat and reserve.

Steam the vegetables separately. Peel the beets while still warm and reserve.

Season the tuna fillets with salt and pepper. Put a large frying pan on high heat. Add the oil to the frying pan. When it reaches smoking point, sear the tuna for 30 seconds on each side. The object is to have a crust on the outside and rare tuna inside.

Warm the shallot reduction, then transfer to a blender. With the blender running on high, add the butter, the raw beet, and the horseradish. Pass through a fine strainer.

Presentation:

Warm six plates. Fold each rösti in half. Lean some steamed vegetables on each rösti. Place a seared tuna fillet beside the vegetables. Pour a small pool of beurre blanc sauce onto each plate. Serve at once.

Barbequed Salmon
with Olive Rissole and Tomatoes

FOR THE RISSOLE:

2 medium potatoes, cooked and peeled

3 Tbsp./45 mL pitted Niçoise or Spanish olives

3 Tbsp./45 mL Roasted Red Peppers (page 155)

1 clove garlic, finely chopped

2 Tbsp./30 mL olive oil for cooking

3 Tbsp./45 mL ripe tomato concassé

Salt and freshly ground black pepper to taste

FOR THE SALMON:

6, 5-oz./140-g fillets fresh salmon, at room
    temperature

Salt to taste

$^1/_2$ tsp./2.5 mL chopped fresh chilies

2 Tbsp./30 mL olive oil for cooking

2 Tbsp./30 mL fresh lemon juice

1 tsp./5 mL fresh summer savory leaves

▶Serves six

Preheat an oven to 400°F/200°C. Dice the cooked potatoes. Dice the olives, peppers, and tomatoes to a uniform size. Sauté the garlic in frying pan with the olive oil. Add the potatoes and place the pan in the oven for 10 minutes. When potatoes are golden brown, add the olives and the peppers. Reserve the tomato concassé. Return the pan to the oven for 10 more minutes, stirring occasionally.

Meanwhile, season the salmon with salt and chilies. Heat a frying pan on high heat and add the cooking olive oil. Sear the salmon for 2 minutes on each side and then place the salmon pan in the oven with the vegetables to finish cooking, about 5 minutes. Remove salmon and vegetables from the oven at the same time.

Presentation:

Warm six dinner plates. Place a salmon fillet on each plate. Sprinkle each fillet with lemon juice. Stir the tomato concassé and the summer savory into the rissole vegetables. Place a mound of the rissole beside each salmon fillet. Serve at once.

Roasted Chicken Breast with Succotash
and Light Sage Sauce

FOR THE SUCCOTASH:

1 buttercup squash

1 lb./455 g fresh, shucked romano or lima beans

1 bay leaf

6 freshly shucked cobs of corn

3 Tbsp./45 mL unsalted butter

Salt and freshly ground black pepper to taste

FOR THE CHICKEN BREASTS:

1 Tbsp./15 mL sunflower oil

6 chicken breasts with skin

Salt and freshly ground black pepper to taste

FOR THE SAUCE:

1/2 cup/120 mL dry white vermouth

1/2 cup/120 mL Chicken Stock (page 14)

4 Tbsp./60 mL 35% whipping cream

1 Tbsp./15 mL roughly chopped fresh sage

▶ Serves six

Preheat an oven to 350°F/175°C. Cut the squash in half and scoop out the seeds. Place the squash on a baking sheet, cover with aluminum foil and bake for 45 minutes or until the flesh is soft.

Meanwhile, rinse the beans in water. Simmer them in unsalted water with the bay leaf until they are soft.

Cut the corn kernels from the cobs by holding the cobs perpendicular to the cutting board and shaving off the kernels with a sharp knife. Reserve.

Remove the squash from the oven. Scoop out spoon-sized pieces of the cooked flesh. Reserve.

Heat the butter in a large frying pan. When it is sizzling add all the vegetables. Sauté gently for 10 minutes. Season and reserve.

Place a large ovenproof frying pan on high heat. Add the sunflower oil. Season the chicken breasts and place them skin side down in the hot oil. Sear for 3 minutes and then turn them over. Roast the chicken breasts in the oven for 15 minutes. Remove the pan from the oven and reserve the chicken breasts on a baking sheet.

Discard the excess oil from the chicken pan. Deglaze with vermouth and chicken stock using a wire whisk to mix in the drippings. Reduce the sauce by 75 percent. Add the cream. Continue to reduce for 2 more minutes. Add the sage and remove from the heat.

Presentation:

Warm six plates. Place a mound of succotash on each plate. Place a chicken breast onto each mound of succotash. Pour a spoonful of sage sauce onto each plate. Serve at once.

My first encounter with succotash was in the freezer section of the grocery store and the "thufferin' thuccotash" of Sylvester the cat in the cartoon. The origin of succotash is in native North American agriculture. Corn, squash, and beans were typically grown as companion crops. The combination of the three vegetables is, therefore, no accident.

Baked Halibut in Duxelles
with White Wine Sauce

Sometimes in order to bring a recipe together at the end, you have to start in the middle and jump around. Bear with me if I jump around a bit with this one.

FOR THE SAUCE:

5 lbs./2.25 kg halibut bones

1 Spanish onion, peeled and sliced

1 leek, sliced and cleaned (white part only)

1 small celery root, peeled and sliced

1 fennel bulb, cleaned and sliced

1 small sprig of tarragon

12 cracked black peppercorns

1, 25-oz./750-mL bottle Riesling or unwooded Chardonnay wine

2 cups/480 mL 35% whipping cream

FOR THE DUXELLES:

1 lb./455 g mushrooms, very finely chopped

1 shallot, peeled and very finely diced

$^1/_2$ cup/120 mL Riesling or unwooded Chardonnay wine

FOR THE VEGETABLE ACCOMPANIMENTS:

2 medium sweet potatoes or yams

2 Tbsp./30 mL olive oil for cooking

1 clove garlic, finely chopped

2 bunches spinach, washed twice

Salt and freshly ground black pepper to taste

FOR THE HALIBUT:

6, 5-oz./140-g fillets fresh halibut

$^1/_4$ cup/60 mL all purpose flour

2 beaten eggs

4 Tbsp./60 mL unsalted butter

▶Serves six

Roughly chop the halibut bones and place them in a large stainless steel pot. Add the rest of the sauce ingredients except the cream. Bring to the boil and reduce heat to a simmer for 30 minutes. Reduce the cream by simmering it in a separate pot to one-quarter of its original volume.

Purée the vegetable mixture in a food processor. Push the purée through a fine sieve. Return it to a clean pot and return to the boil. Reduce this to half of its original volume. Mix into the reduced cream. Continue to reduce until it reaches sauce consistency. Season with salt and pepper and reserve.

Preheat an oven to 350°F/175°C. Place the chopped mushrooms and shallot on a baking sheet. Douse with the wine and place in the oven. Stir regularly for 45 minutes or until almost all the liquid has evaporated. When finished, the duxelles should resemble damp breadcrumbs.

Put the sweet potatoes on another tray in

the oven at the same time for approximately the same amount of time as the duxelles. The sweet potatoes are ready when the flesh yields to a skewer inserted during the roasting. Remove the sweet potatoes from the oven and peel them when they are cool enough to handle.

"Bread" the fillets of halibut by first dredging them in the flour, then dipping them in the beaten egg and finally coating them in the mushroom duxelles. Reserve.

Slice 12 discs of sweet potato and place them on a baking sheet in the oven to keep warm.

Heat the olive oil and garlic in a frying pan and sauté the spinach for about 2 minutes. Season and keep the spinach warm in the oven with the sweet potatoes.

Heat the butter in a large frying pan. When it is sizzling add the halibut fillets. Cook them for about 3 minutes on each side.

Presentation:

Warm six plates. Arrange two slices of sweet potato and a spoonful of spinach on each plate. Place a fillet of halibut beside the vegetables. Ladle a small pool of the sauce beside the fish. Serve at once.

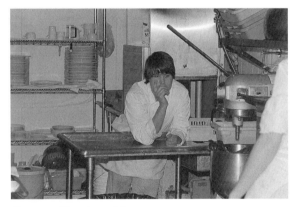
Dave waiting to get busy.

With Lam, catering.

Spicy Salad with Grilled Beef
and Toasted Peanuts

FOR THE MARINADE:

2 Tbsp./30 mL soy sauce

1 Tbsp./15 mL honey

1 tsp./5 mL finely chopped green chilies

1 Tbsp./15 mL fresh lemon juice

1 Tbsp./15 mL sunflower oil

1 clove garlic, finely chopped

FOR THE SALAD:

1 head Boston lettuce

1 head red leaf lettuce

1 head romaine lettuce

FOR THE BEEF:

2, 10-oz./285-g well-marbled rib eye or striploin
   steaks

Salt to taste

FOR THE GARNISH:

$^1/_3$ lb./140 g peanuts, shelled, roasted, and skinned

▶Serves six

Combine all the ingredients for the marinade in a stainless steel bowl. Start the barbeque. Wash the lettuces and tear them into small pieces. Thoroughly dry the leaves.

Season the steaks and grill them to your preference. Let the steaks cool slightly on the cutting board before slicing each steak into thin strips and placing the strips in the marinade.

Presentation:

Place a mound of salad greens on each plate. Drape slices of beef on the salad. Sprinkle each plate with toasted peanuts. Spoon excess marinade onto each salad. Serve at once.

Mustard Pork with Marjoram
and Sweet Onions

FOR THE PORK:

¼ cup/60 mL Dijon mustard

1 clove garlic, finely chopped

2 lbs./900 g pork neck

1 tsp./5 mL roughly chopped rosemary

Salt and freshly ground black pepper to taste

FOR THE ONIONS:

2 Tbsp./30 mL red wine vinegar

Salt and freshly ground black pepper to taste

1 medium sweet onion (Vidalia, for example)

1 tsp./5 mL roughly chopped marjoram

▶ Serves six

Measure the mustard, garlic, and rosemary into a stainless steel bowl. Cut the pork across the grain into six equal slices. Pound the slices between sheets of plastic with the bottom of a saucepan or with a meat pounder. Pound each piece as thinly as possible without tearing. Add the slices to the mustard mixture and coat well.

While the meat is marinating, start the barbeque. Combine the red wine vinegar with salt and pepper. Next, slice the onion across the grain into very thin slices and place in the vinegar mixture.

Grill the pork slices on the barbeque for 2 minutes on each side.

Presentation:

Warm a serving platter. Transfer the pork slices to the platter. Arrange slices of marinated onions on top of the pork. Sprinkle with marjoram.

Warm Apricot Millefeuille

2/3 cup/160 mL sugar plus 1/4 cup/60 mL

3 cups/720 mL pitted and halved fresh apricots

1 lb./455 g Puff Pastry (page 23) or frozen

1 lb./455 g almond paste

1 beaten egg

Whipped cream for garnish, optional

▶Serves six

Mix 2/3 cup/160 mL sugar and apricots in a stainless steel bowl. Pour into a colander to drain.

Divide the pastry in half. Roll one half to a length of 12 inches/30 cm, a width of 4 inches/10 cm and a thickness of 1/4 inch/.6 cm. Roll the pastry up onto the rolling pin and unroll it onto a baking sheet lined with parchment paper. Divide the almond paste in half and roll one half as long as the first layer of puff pastry, but not quite as wide. Roll it up onto the rolling pin and unroll it directly onto the first layer of puff pastry. Mound the drained apricots evenly over the surface of the almond paste.

Cover the apricots with another layer of rolled-out almond paste. Paint a light coating of beaten egg around the perimeter of the first layer of puff pastry to help the final layer of puff pastry adhere to the first. Cover the almond paste with the final layer of rolled-out puff pastry. Crimp the pastry where the top and bottom layers of puff pastry join.

Refrigerate the baking sheet with finished pastry on it for 1 hour. Preheat an oven to 325°F/165°C. Take the pastry out of the fridge. Lightly paint the surface of the pastry with beaten egg. Sprinkle the surface liberally with sugar and bake for 45 minutes. Cool for 30 minutes before serving.

Presentation:

Place a slice of pastry on each plate. Garnish with some whipped cream if you like and serve while still slightly warm.

Café Glacé

2 cups/480 mL very strong coffee or espresso

2 cups/480 mL vanilla ice cream, home made
   or store bought

1 Tbsp./15 mL Tia Maria liqueur, optional

1 Tbsp./15 mL sambuca, optional

1/2 cup/120 mL 35% whipping cream

12 roasted coffee beans

▶ Serves six

Refrigerate six parfait glasses or sundae
glasses. Make the coffee and chill it. Churn the
ice cream and scoop it into a large stainless
steel bowl. Pour the coffee into the bowl in a
slow steady stream, while whisking with a wire
whisk. The resulting mixture should resemble
a very thick milkshake. Adjust the flavor with
the liqueurs. In another bowl, whip the whipping cream.

Presentation:

Take the sundae glasses out of the fridge. Spoon
the coffee mixture into each glass. Spoon a
little dollop of whipped cream on top of each
glass. Garnish with a couple of roasted coffee
beans. Serve at once.

Vanilla and Raspberry Sandwich

I like to draw recipe ideas from the collective unconscious. Sometimes the ideas are whimsical. This one comes from the ice cream sandwich, that everyone remembers from their school cafeteria days or their corner store.

The gelatin leaves that are called for in this recipe are available in gourmet food shops.

FOR THE SAUCE AND GARNISH:

3 cups/720 mL fresh raspberries

1/2 cup/120 mL sugar

FOR THE CHOCOLATE WAFERS:

1 recipe Chocolate Wafer Batter (page 25)

FOR THE VANILLA MOUSSE:

1 fresh vanilla bean, split in half

2/3 cup/160 mL sugar

3 gelatin leaves

6 egg yolks

2 egg whites

1 3/4 cups/420 mL 35% whipping cream

Icing sugar in a shaker

▶Serves six

Go to a hardware or building supply store and purchase a 2-foot/60-cm length of 3-inch/7.5 cm PVC pipe. Ask to have it cut into six, 3-inch/7.5-cm pieces. These are the molds for assembling this dessert. Find a plastic yogourt container lid and, using a sharp craft knife, cut out a circle exactly the same diameter as the interior of the PVC pieces. This rim will serve as the template for your chocolate discs. Find another yogourt lid and, using a heated metal skewer, puncture/melt a series of holes in a circular pattern. This series of punctures will serve as the template for garnishing the chocolate discs with icing sugar. Now all the special tools required for this recipe are ready.

Slice half of the raspberries in half lengthwise with a sharp knife. Refrigerate. Purée the rest of the raspberries in a blender with the sugar and pass through a fine sieve. Reserve.

Preheat an oven to 350°F/175°C. Turn a baking sheet upside down and grease lightly with butter. Place the chocolate wafer template (yogourt lid) on the baking sheet and place a little batter inside the template. Use a spatula or palette knife to evenly distribute the batter. Move the template around on the tray, leaving some room between circles of batter, and repeat to form 18 circles. Bake the wafer batter for 10 minutes or until the discs have set and the edges have browned slightly. Remove the baked discs and cool them on a wire rack.

Scrape the interior of the vanilla pod to separate the gummy substance from the husk. Combine the resinous gum with 2/3 cup/160 mL of sugar. In a separate bowl soak the gelatin leaves in cold water. Mix the vanilla sugar with the egg yolks in a stainless steel bowl. Whisk over a pot of boiling water to make a sabayon.

Squeeze out the gelatin leaves and add them to the sabayon while it is still warm. Whisk the egg whites in a separate bowl until stiff. Fold the whites into the sabayon. Whip the cream and fold it into the sabayon. Refrigerate. Now the vanilla mousse is ready and you may begin to assemble the dessert.

Line a baking sheet with waxed paper. Place the six PVC molds on the waxed paper. Drop a chocolate disc into each mold. Line the interior of each mold with the halved raspberries, cut side facing out. Spoon some of the mousse mixture into each mold to the height of the top of the raspberry halves. Drop another chocolate disc on the mousse. Repeat, finishing with a chocolate disc. Place completed sandwiches in the refrigerator to set for 2 hours.

Presentation:

Run a paring knife around the inside of each mold to release the sandwiches onto six plates. Place the icing sugar template over each sandwich and sprinkle liberally with icing sugar. Lift the template away to reveal several dots of icing sugar.

Pour a small pool of raspberry sauce on the base of each plate, around the sandwiches. Serve at once.

Lauren at Palmerston.

Peach Tarte Tatin with Butter Pecan Ice Cream

FOR THE PASTRY:
12 oz./340 g Sweet Pastry (page 24)

FOR THE PEACHES:
6 large fresh peaches

FOR THE ICE CREAM:
1 recipe Crème Anglaise (page 19)
1/2 lb./225 g shelled pecan halves

1 Tbsp./15 mL butter
Salt to taste

FOR THE CARAMEL:
1 cup/240 mL sugar
1/2 cup/120 mL water
1/4 cup/60 mL butter
1/4 cup/60 mL 35% whipping cream

▶Serves six

Roll out the sweet pastry to a thickness of 1/4 inch/.6 cm. Use a 5-inch/12.5-cm round cutter to cut out six rounds. Place a small sheet of waxed paper between each round and refrigerate.

Cut each peach in half and remove the pit. Cut each half into four wedges. Refrigerate.

Preheat an oven to 350°F/175°C. Make the crème anglaise according to the recipe and refrigerate. Meanwhile, toast the pecan halves, butter, and salt on a baking sheet for 10 minutes. Remove and cool in the refrigerator. Churn the crème anglaise in an ice cream maker. When it is ice cream, fold in the toasted pecans and store in the freezer.

Place the sugar and water in a very clean copper or stainless steel pot over high heat. Boil rapidly without stirring or interruption

until the liquid starts to give off a caramel aroma and begins to turn a medium amber color. If it starts to smoke it has gone too far. Discard and try again. (Remember, the worst kitchen burns come from accidents with caramel. Please be careful with this very hot substance.) When the caramel has reached medium amber, remove the pot from the heat and start stirring in the remaining butter, then the cream. Stir thoroughly. Place the pot back on low heat and begin to make the peach tarte tatins.

Place two, 6-inch/15-cm nonstick frying pans over medium heat. Spoon 2 Tbsp./30 mL of the caramel mixture into each pan. Arrange eight slices of peach in a pleasing pattern on the caramel in the pan. Place a disc of sweet pastry on top. Bake for 15 minutes or until the pastry is golden. Remove from the oven and immediately invert onto a dessert plate. The tarte tatin should be peach side up on the plate. Repeat this process until you have six tarte tatins on six plates.

Presentation:

Lower the temperature in the oven to warm. Warm the six plates with the tartes on them briefly. Remove and place a generous scoop of ice cream in the center of each tarte. Serve at once.

Gail Yacula in 1989.

Organic Yogourt with Fruit and Honey

6 cups/1.5 litres organic yogourt

6 Tbsp./90 mL Blackberry Purée (page 114)

6 ripe peaches, washed

1 cup/240 mL raspberries, washed

1 cup/240 mL wild blueberries, washed

6 Tbsp./90 mL liquid honey

3 Tbsp./45 mL toasted hazelnuts

▶Serves six

Place the yogourt in a sieve lined with cheese-cloth over a stainless steel bowl. Refrigerate overnight. The following day transfer the drained yogourt to a stainless steel bowl. Mix the Blackberry Purée with the yogourt. Cut the peaches into sixths.

Presentation:

Divide the yogourt among six bowls. Arrange the peaches and the berries on the yogourt. Drizzle with honey. Sprinkle with roughly chopped hazelnuts. Serve at once.

Feast of Fields.

Summer Fruit Salad with Golden Plum Sorbet

FOR THE SORBET:

4 cups/950 mL ripe golden plums

Sugar to taste

FOR THE FRUIT SALAD:

3 ripe peaches

3 ripe plums

3 ripe apricots

1 cup/240 mL wild blueberries

1 cup/240 mL raspberries

1 cup/240 mL strawberries

1 bunch fresh mint

▶ Serves six

Wash the golden plums. Split them in half and place them in a stainless steel pot. Start with 1 cup of sugar and gently simmer the split plums, with their pits, covered, for approximately 15 minutes. Stir often and taste for sweetness. The flavor should be tart, and not so sweet as to override the fruit flavor. Purée in a food processor and pass through a fine sieve. Churn in an ice cream maker and store in the freezer.

Meanwhile, wash and cut all the fruit, except the berries, into wedges. Wash and hull the strawberries and cut into halves or quarters. Add the raspberries and blueberries whole. Toss all the fruit with a sprinkling of sugar. This helps to get the juices running.

Presentation:

Ladle some fruit into each of six wide bowls. Place a dollop of sorbet on top. Garnish with a mint sprig. Serve at once.

Lemon Curd Tart
with Wild Blueberry Compote

FOR THE PASTRY:
1 lb./455 g Sweet Pastry (page 24)

FOR THE LEMON FILLING:
6 whole eggs
6 egg yolks

1¼ cups/300 mL sugar
1¼ cups/300 mL lemon juice
6 tsp./30 mL blanched lemon zest
1¼ cups/300 mL butter

FOR THE GARNISH:
1 cup/240 mL Wild Blueberry Compote (page 113)

▶Serves six

Preheat an oven to 350°F/175°C. Roll out the sweet pastry to a thickness of ⅛ inch/.3 cm. Roll the dough over the rolling pin and drape it over a 10-inch/25-cm pie dish or a similarly sized scalloped tart form with a removable bottom. Blind bake the pastry for 30 minutes or until golden brown.

   Place all the ingredients for the lemon curd in a stainless steel pot. Place the pot over medium heat and stir until the mixture thickens. The mixture will thicken below boiling point so try not to let it boil. If the mixture boils, the butter could separate and cause the filling to have a greasy appearance. When the mixture has thickened, remove it from the heat and stir vigorously, then pour it immediately into the prebaked tart shell. Cool for 15 minutes at room temperature and then refrigerate for 2 hours before serving.

Presentation:
Place a wedge of lemon tart on each of six dessert plates. Garnish with 1 Tbsp./15 mL of Wild Blueberry Compote. Serve.

Raspberry Tart with Chocolate Shake

FOR THE PASTRY:

1 lb./455 g Sweet Pastry (page 24)

FOR THE FILLING:

3 cups/720 mL fresh raspberries

3/4 cup/180 mL Crème Fraîche, sweet variation
  (page 19)

FOR THE CHOCOLATE SHAKE:

4 cups/950 mL milk

3 cups/720 mL chocolate ice cream

This is like getting two desserts!

▶ Serves six

Preheat an oven to 350°F/175°C. Roll out the dough to a 1/8-inch/.3-cm thickness. Roll it up onto the rolling pin and drape it over a scalloped 10-inch/25-cm tart form with a removable bottom. Blind bake for 30 minutes or until golden brown.

Crush one-third of the raspberries with a fork and mix with the sweet crème fraîche. Spread this mixture evenly over the base of the prebaked tart form. Place the remaining raspberries, tightly together, on the cream mixture,

facing up. There should be barely any cream visible beneath them. Chill.

Place the milk and ice cream in a blender and purée to make milkshakes.

Presentation:

Place a wedge of raspberry tart on each of six plates. Pour the chocolate milkshake into six tall glasses. Place a glass beside each plate. Serve at once.

Chocolate Beignets

FOR THE CREPES:

4 eggs

3 Tbsp./45 mL melted butter

2 cups/480 mL milk, at room temperature

1 cup/240 mL sifted pastry flour

1 orange, grated rind

1/4 tsp./1.2 mL salt

FOR CHOCOLATE GANACHE:

1 cup/240 mL bittersweet chocolate

3/4 cup/180 mL 35% whipping cream

2 Tbsp./30 mL Grand Marnier liqueur

FOR THE FRYING BATTER:

1/2 cup/120 mL beer

3 egg yolks

1/4 tsp./1.2 mL salt

1/3 cup/80 mL sifted pastry flour

3 egg whites

4 cups/950 mL sunflower oil

2 cups/480 mL sugar

FOR THE GARNISH:

1 cup/240 mL 35% whipping cream

1/2 cup/120 mL fresh raspberries

▶Serves six

Combine the crepe ingredients, except the flour, in a stainless steel bowl. Sift the flour into the bowl and gently combine. Let the batter sit for 1 hour before use.

Break the chocolate into small pieces. Scald the cream and remove from heat. Stir the chocolate pieces and the Grand Marnier into the hot cream until smooth. Chill overnight.

Use nonstick 7-inch/18-cm frying pans to produce the crepes. Try to use two pans at once. This way the crepes will be ready twice as fast. It will take a couple of tries to get the heat adjusted properly to make nice crepes, but don't worry, there is plenty of batter. You will

need 12 crepes for this recipe. Store excess crepes in the freezer for another time.

Place prepared crepes on the counter. Place 1 Tbsp./15 mL ganache in the center of each crepe. Wrap the crepe around each mound of ganache to form 12 separate packages. Refrigerate.

Measure the beer, egg yolks, and salt into a stainless steel bowl. Mix in sifted pastry flour. Do not overmix. In a separate bowl, whisk the egg whites until stiff peaks form. Fold the egg whites into the egg yolk mixture. Pour the oil into a stainless steel stockpot and set over high heat until the oil reaches 350°F/175°C. Reduce heat to simmer.

Coat the chocolate packages with the frying batter and fry them in batches, being careful not to crowd them in the oil. Agitate the packages as they fry. Lift the packages out of the oil with a slotted spoon when they are golden brown. Drain them on paper towels and then roll them in sugar.

Whip the cream to soft peaks.

Presentation:

Place a dollop of softly whipped cream on each of six plates. Drizzle some raspberry purée on each dollop of whipped cream. Place two beignets on each plate. Serve while still warm.

Ken Steele (far right) with the men and women of Superior.

JK ROM *kitchen staff before a big gig.*

Whisky-Poached Peach with Almond Cookie

This recipe may be prepared as a single batch to end a summer repast or it may be made in a larger quantity to be preserved for use throughout the year.

FOR THE PEACHES:

3 cups/720 mL water

6 large peaches, ripe but firm

1 cup/240 mL sugar

1 split vanilla bean

1/3 cup/80 mL bourbon whisky

FOR THE ALMOND COOKIE:

1 cup/240 mL Sweet Pastry (page 24)

1 cup/240 mL whole almonds

▶ Serves six

Bring the water to the boil. Dip the peaches in one at a time for 30 seconds or long enough to loosen the skins. Add the sugar to the water and bring back to the boil. Add the vanilla bean and reduce to a simmer. Add the whisky and the peaches and cover for 1 hour.

Preheat an oven to 350°F/175°C. Toast the almonds for 10 minutes or until slightly colored inside. Cool for 30 minutes at room temperature. Crush with a mallet or by using the pulse mode in a food processor.

To make the cookies, "dust" the rolling sur-face with crushed almonds. Roll the sweet pastry right on the almonds. Keep adding almonds as you roll until the pastry is 1/3 inch/.85 cm thick. Cut out shapes using a cookie cutter and transfer to a baking sheet. Chill the cookies for 30 minutes before baking. Bake for 10 minutes or until golden.

Presentation:

Place a whole poached peach in each of six bowls. Spoon some of the whisky syrup into each bowl. Serve with a platter of cookies.

Summer Fruits in Rum

This recipe originates in Germany, where it is called "rumtopf." I learned it from my friend Michael Stadtländer. It is the sort of preserve that one keeps adding to as the summer season progresses. A special touch is the addition of a green walnut in late summer or early autumn. The green husk surrounding the unripe walnut is extremely aromatic and adds an interesting note to the mixture of fruits in rum.

Start with a glazed earthenware jar with a lid. Place a layer of washed and hulled strawberries on the bottom. Sprinkle some sugar on the strawberries. Pour rum on the strawberries until they are half covered. Place the jar in the refrigerator until raspberries come into season. Repeat the process with raspberries, red currants, gooseberries, sour cherries, wild blueberries, and blackberries. In late August add one green walnut. Give the fruits a gentle stir and place the pot in the refrigerator until late December. Serve as an accompaniment to cake or ice cream.

Ideally, this batch of fruits in rum will last you until next December when your new batch will be ready.

Apricots in Vanilla Syrup

3 cups/720 mL sugar
13 cups/3 litres water

6 lbs./1.7 kg apricots, ripe but firm
6 fresh vanilla beans

▶ Yields six, 1-quart/ 1-litre jars

Sterilize jars and prepare seals according to directions on package. Boil the sugar and water together to make the syrup. Wash the apricots, split them in half lengthwise, and remove the pits. Place a split vanilla bean into each jar. Pack the apricots into the jars as compactly as possible. Pour the syrup over the fruit and fill to the neck of each jar. Place a seal and crown on each jar and place the jars in a large pot. Cover the jars with water and bring to a boil. Boil for 20 minutes. Remove. The jars will seal as they cool.

Although this recipe is for apricots, several other seasonal summer fruits may be substituted with excellent results. Try the same recipe with any type of plum, black cherries, or sugar pears.

Pickled Jardinière Vegetables

The specific vegetables used in this recipe can vary according to your taste. I like to use vegetables that will create some color contrast in the jar and flavor contrast on the palate. We usually make this recipe in early July when there are enough local vegetables in season to get started.

FOR THE VEGETABLES:

1 lb./455 g peeled young carrots

1 lb./455 g cauliflower, broken into small florets, washed

1 lb./455 g trimmed green beans, washed

1 lb./455 g trimmed yellow beans, washed

1 lb./455 g peeled pearl onions

1 lb./455 g shucked romano beans

FOR PICKLING LIQUID OR BRINE:

8 cups/2 litres water

2 Tbsp./30 mL sea salt

4 cups/950 mL white wine vinegar

1 tsp./5 mL powdered turmeric

12 whole black peppercorns

1 tsp./5 mL whole mustard seeds

1 tsp./5 mL whole coriander seeds

▶ Yields six, 1-quart/1-litre jars

Preheat an oven to 350°F/175°C. Place six quart or litre preserving jars in the oven for 15 minutes. Follow the directions on the package for preparing the seals for use.

When the jars are cool, pack them as tightly as possible with an assortment of all the vegetables.

Simmer the brine mixture for 15 minutes and pour over the vegetables in the jar.

Seal and process the jars up to their necks in boiling water for 20 minutes. Remove the jars to the counter to cool. As they cool they will form a seal. Keep them in a cool, dark place for use throughout the year.

Wild Blueberry Compote

6 lbs./2.7 kg wild blueberries

12 Tbsp./180 mL sugar

▶ Yields six, 1-quart/1-litre jars

Sterilize six quart- or litre-sized jars and prepare seals according to the directions on the package. Wash the blueberries and place them in a stainless steel pot with the sugar. Bring to the boil, stirring from time to time, and cook for five minutes. Pour the hot mixture into the sterilized jars. Place the seals and crowns on the jars.

The jars will seal as they cool. This method of sealing is called "hot pack."

Peaches in Bourbon Whisky

10 lbs./4.5 kg firm, ripe freestone peaches
13 cups/3 litres Syrup (page 111)

12 Tbsp./180 mL bourbon whisky

Yields six, 1-quart/1-litre jars

Sterilize six quart- or litre-sized jars and prepare seals according to the directions on the package. Bring a large saucepan of water to the boil. Plunge the peaches into the water for approximately 30 seconds to loosen their skins. Then remove the skins and split the peaches in half. Remove the pits and pack the peaches as compactly as possible into the jars. Add 2 Tbsp./30 mL bourbon whisky to each jar. Add the syrup to each jar. Place a seal and crown on each jar. Process as for apricots (page 111).

There are several varieties of peaches grown. Freestone peaches are better suited for canning and clingstone peaches are usually better for eating fresh.

Blackberry Purée

2 quarts/2 litres blackberries
2 cups/480 mL sugar

¹/₂ cup/120 mL water

▶Yields 3 pints/300 mL

Sterilize three pint or ¹/₂-litre jars and prepare seals according to the directions on the package. Put all the ingredients in a stainless steel pot and bring to a boil. Reduce heat and simmer, covered, for 15 minutes. Pass through a fine strainer into three pint-sized/¹/₂-litre jars. Cover each jar with a seal and crown and process in boiling water for 15 minutes.

Black Currant Purée

The aroma of fresh black currants is intoxicating. This purée can be mixed with white wine to make a delicious aperitif or with sparkling water for a refreshing non-alcoholic beverage.

2 quarts/2 litres fresh black currants
1 cup/240 mL Riesling wine

¹/₂ cup/120 mL honey

▶Yields 3 pints/300 mL

Sterilize three pint or ¹/₂-litre jars and prepare seals according to the directions on the package. Pour the black currants into a stainless steel pot. Add the wine and honey and bring to the boil. Reduce heat to simmer and cover. Simmer, covered, for 15 minutes. Pass through a fine strainer and transfer purée to pint-sized/¹/₂-litre jars. Top the jars with sealers and crowns and process in boiling water for 15 minutes.

Pickled Beets

4 quarts/4 litres young beets (roots attached)

2 Tbsp./30 mL whole allspice

2 sticks whole cinnamon

6 cups/1.5 litres cider vinegar

1 tsp./5 mL whole mustard seed

1/2 cup/120 mL honey

▶ Yields 8 pints/800 mL

Sterilize eight pint or 1/2-litre jars and prepare seals according to the directions on the package. Cook the beets in salted water for 40 minutes or until their skins come off easily when pinched. Drain, and peel the beets when they are cool enough to handle. Leave the beets whole or, if they are too large, cut them into quarters. Pack the beets into pint-sized/1/2-litre jars. Combine the rest of the ingredients in a stainless steel pan and warm to simmering point. Mix well and ladle liquid over the beets up to the necks of the bottles. Cover each jar with a seal and crown and process in boiling water for 15 minutes.

Anne Rumble at Feast of Fields.

Anne and Julia at Feast of Fields.

Ken and Margaret in the kitchen at JK ROM.

Fall

During service at JK ROM.

Reggiano Twists

Any number of dry, aged cheeses could be substituted for Parmigiano Reggiano in this recipe, although it has the most appeal.

1/3 cup/80 mL freshly grated Parmigiano Reggiano

1 tsp./5 mL paprika

1/2 lb./225 g Puff Pastry (page 23)

▶Serves six

Preheat an oven to 350°F/175°C. Sprinkle a rolling surface with a mixture of the grated cheese and paprika. Roll out the pastry on the cheese and paprika so that it is thoroughly imbedded in the pastry. Roll the pastry out to a 1/4-inch/.6-cm thickness. Cut the pastry into strips approximately 5 inches/12.5 cm long and 1/2 inch/1.2 cm wide. Twist the pastry and roll each strip briefly on the counter with the palms of your hands to form straw-shaped cylinders with a twist in them. Place the straws on a baking sheet and refrigerate for 30 minutes. Bake for 5 minutes or until the twists puff up and turn golden-brown.

Presentation:

Stack the twists log cabin-style on a plate. Serve them to your guests with fino sherry or any other refreshing beverage.

Grilled Lamb Cevapcici

This hors d'oeuvre hails from Yugoslavia. There, I am told by my friend Steve Stefancic, it is actually sold as street food by vendors with portable barbeques, and served with ajvar, a condiment made with roasted red peppers and eggplant.

1 lb./455 g freshly ground lamb

2 cloves garlic, finely chopped

1 tsp./5 mL roughly chopped rosemary

1/4 cup/60 mL Roasted Red Peppers (page 155)

Salt and freshly ground black pepper to taste

▶Serves six

Combine all the ingredients in a stainless steel bowl. Form cylindrical patties approximately 2 inches/5 cm long. When they are formed, grill them on a charcoal or gas barbeque.

Presentation:

You may skewer the finished patties on bamboo skewers or serve them on a plate. Either way, they are meant to be finger food.

Wild Mushroom Fritters

4 cups/950 mL sunflower oil

1 cup/240 mL sliced white mushrooms

1 cup/240 mL roughly torn oyster mushrooms

1 cup/240 mL sliced shiitake mushroom caps

1/4 cup/60 mL peeled and sliced shallot

3 egg whites

1/4 cup/60 mL roughly chopped Italian parsley

4 Tbsp./60 mL all purpose flour

Salt to taste

▶ Serves six

Measure the oil into a large stockpot and heat to 350°F/175°C. Meanwhile, prepare the mushrooms and other vegetables. Whip the egg whites until they form soft peaks. Fold all the other ingredients into the whipped egg whites. Form balls and drop them carefully into the oil. Turn often in the oil. Remove with a slotted spoon when they are golden all over. Drain on paper towels.

Presentation:

Place fritters on a plate and serve while they are still hot.

Wayne, Victoria, Lance, Andy, and Michelle before a big gig.

Salt Cod and Olives on Crisp Toast

Society has evolved since the days of the triangle trade: slaves for rum and salt cod. However, vestiges of that trade remain. Travel to the Caribbean and you may be puzzled to find that, even though the waters surrounding the islands are teeming with fish, the local cuisines feature dishes like "Saltfish and Ackee." Salt cod remains a staple in European countries as well. In Portugal, it is referred to as "mountain fish" because of its ability to travel inland and keep "fresh" indefinitely.

For this dish, it will be necessary to start the preparation 36 hours before serving.

FOR THE SALT COD:

$^1/_2$ lb./228 g salt cod

2 medium potatoes

1 clove garlic, finely chopped

$^1/_4$ cup/60 mL fine olive oil

Freshly ground black pepper to taste

FOR THE OLIVE TOASTS:

12 slices white or whole wheat bread

$^1/_2$ cup/120 mL small Niçoise or Italian olives

1 small tomato, washed

2 Tbsp./30 mL fine olive oil

▶ Serves six

Place the cod in a pot big enough to completely submerge it in water. Soak the cod in several changes of water for 24 hours. The soaking leaches out most of the salt and also rehydrates the fish so that it approximates the look and feel of fresh cod. After 24 hours, remove the fish from the water and set on towels to drain.

Boil the potatoes in salted water until soft. Flake the cod with your fingers into a stainless steel bowl. Add the chopped garlic. Working with a fork, add the olive oil while mashing the cod mixture.

When the potatoes are cooked, peel them and mash them into the cod mixture. Adjust seasoning with black pepper.

Preheat an oven to 275°F/135°C. Cut the crusts off the bread and slice the bread into squares or triangles. Place the shapes on a baking sheet and bake in the oven for 20 minutes or until they are crunchy and golden.

Roughly chop the olives and tomato and mix with the olive oil.

Presentation:

Spread some of the cod mixture on each piece of toast. Spoon some of the olive-tomato mixture on each canapé and serve on a platter.

Crispy Artichoke Salad
with Tomato and Roasted Red Pepper Fondue

FOR THE SALAD:

2 bunches arugula

1 head Boston lettuce

6 cherry tomatoes

FOR THE TOMATO/PEPPER PURÉE:

3 tomatoes, washed

2 Roasted Red Peppers (page 155)

Salt and freshly ground black pepper

FOR THE ARTICHOKES:

$1/2$ cup/120 mL olive oil for cooking

3 artichokes

2 Tbsp./30 mL fine olive oil

▶ Serves six

Wash the arugula and the Boston lettuce in two changes of water. Spin dry. Wash the cherry tomatoes. Reserve in the refrigerator.

Preheat an oven to 350°F/175°C. Cut the tomatoes in half and place them cut side up on a baking sheet. Sprinkle with salt and black pepper. Roast in the oven for 30 minutes or until they are shrivelled. Take them out of the oven and transfer to a food processor. Add the roasted red peppers and purée. Pass through a fine strainer and discard seeds. Reserve.

Heat the cooking olive oil in a stainless steel pot to 350°F/175°C. Remove outer leaves of artichokes and cut the artichokes into quarters lengthwise. Pare away the fibrous "choke" from the artichoke and cut the quarters in half. When you are finished you should have 24 pieces. Fry the artichoke pieces in the olive oil until they are crisp and golden. Remove them from the oil and place them on paper towels to drain.

Presentation:

Ladle a small pool of tomato fondue in the center of each of six plates. Toss the arugula and Boston lettuce in a salad bowl with the fine olive oil. Season to taste with salt and pepper. Place a mound of salad on the fondue on each plate. Slice the cherry tomatoes in half and place on each salad. Place four pieces of artichoke around the salad on each plate. Serve at once.

Corn and Potato Pancakes
with Tomato Relish

To cut kernels from the cob, hold the cob perpendicular to the cutting surface and, using a sharp knife, slowly carve the kernels of corn from the cob. They will tumble to the cutting surface.

FOR THE PANCAKES:

1 cup/240 mL fresh corn kernels (see Note)

2 potatoes

2 eggs

3 Tbsp./45 mL corn oil

Salt and freshly ground black pepper to taste

$^1/_4$ cup/60 mL sifted pastry flour

FOR THE RELISH:

2 ripe tomatoes

1 red onion

1 clove garlic

2 Tbsp./30 mL roughly chopped fresh basil

$^1/_2$ Tbsp./7.5 mL white wine vinegar

Salt and freshly ground black pepper to taste

▶Serves six

Gather and measure the kernels after cutting them from each cob. Place the corn kernels in a stainless steel mixing bowl. Peel two potatoes (Yukon Gold are the most attractive). Grate them into a separate bowl. Squeeze out excess water before adding to the corn kernels. Add the eggs and corn oil. Blend thoroughly. Add the salt and pepper, then the sifted pastry flour. Do not overmix. Let the batter sit for 30 minutes before making pancakes.

Cut the tomatoes in half and squeeze out the seeds. Dice the tomatoes to approximately the size of corn kernels and put them in a stainless

steel bowl. Repeat with the red onion. Chop the garlic as finely as possible and add it with the vinegar and basil. Adjust the seasoning with salt and pepper.

Preheat an oven to 250°F/120°C. Make six large pancakes in a nonstick frying pan. Keep them warm on a tray in the oven.

Presentation:

Lay out six warm plates. Place a pancake on each plate. Spread a thick layer of relish on each pancake. Serve at once.

Autumn Antipasti

1 quart/litre jar Roasted Red Peppers (page 155)
1 quart/litre jar Marinated Eggplant (page 157)
1 celery root
1 Tbsp./15 mL Mayonnaise (page 18)
Salt and lemon juice to taste

3 ripe tomatoes
Coarse-grained salt and freshly ground black pepper
1/2 lb./227 g Parmigiano Reggiano
18 arugula leaves
Fine olive oil
Salt and freshly ground black pepper to taste

▶ Serves six

Drain the peppers and eggplant, reserving their packing liquid. Peel the celery root and slice it into julienne. Dress with mayonnaise and adjust seasoning with the salt and lemon juice. Reserve.

Slice the tomatoes into quarters. Season with coarse salt and black pepper. Reserve. Use a paring knife to make shards of Parmesan cheese. Reserve. Wash and dry the arugula. Season with olive oil, salt, and pepper.

Presentation:

Arrange the ingredients on each plate separately, in an interesting and appetizing pattern. Alternatively, arrange on larger platters for a buffet.

This recipe is an opportunity to use some of your preserves from the summer and autumn. Present them in a simple way, either as a plated first course or on a platter. Use your imagination in the ingredients that you choose. I find that presenting an odd number of items usually looks more appealing. Use contrasting colors when possible as well. This is a combination of preserves that I like to use.

Fall Greens with Pickled Peppers
and Fine Olive Oil

¹/₂ head escarole

1 small head radicchio

1 Belgian endive

12 leaves arugula

3 Tbsp./45 mL fine olive oil

1 Tbsp./15 mL liquid from Pickled Tomato Peppers

Salt and freshly ground black pepper to taste

1 quart/litre jar Pickled Tomato Peppers (page 155)

▶Serves six

Break the salad leaves into small pieces and wash them in two changes of water. Spin dry. Transfer lettuces to a salad bowl. Toss with the oil, pickling liquid, and seasonings. Cut the tomato peppers in quarters.

Presentation:

Mound the dressed greens on each of six plates. Garnish with three-quarters of pickled tomato peppers.

David Pell at JK ROM.

Smoky Chanterelle Salad with Tomatoes

2 Tbsp./30 mL olive oil for cooking

2 shallots, peeled and finely chopped

1/4 cup/60 mL bacon lardons

1 lb./455 g chanterelles (see page 74)

1 Tbsp./15 mL chopped Italian parsley

1 tsp./5 mL fresh thyme leaves

Salt and freshly ground black pepper to taste

18 fresh spinach leaves

6 medium ripe tomatoes, washed

2 Tbsp./30 mL fine olive oil

▶ Serves six

Heat the olive oil in a large frying pan over medium high heat. Add the shallots and bacon. Sauté gently for 5 minutes. Brush the dust from the chanterelles and add them to the shallots and bacon. Sauté for an additional 5 minutes. Add the parsley, thyme, salt, and pepper. Remove from heat. Add the spinach leaves and toss to wilt the spinach.

Slice the tomatoes into rounds. Sprinkle with salt and pepper and olive oil.

Presentation:

Arrange tomato slices on each plate in a circular overlapping pattern leaving a hole in the middle. Spoon the chanterelle mixture in the center of each plate. Drizzle the tomatoes with fine olive oil. Serve at once.

Wild Mushroom Strudel with Riesling Sauce

This recipe is an opportunity to experiment with making your own strudel dough. The fallback position is to purchase filo pastry from the grocery store.

FOR THE FILLING:

1/2 loaf white bread, crusts removed

1/2 cup/120 mL milk

3 shallots, peeled and cut into brunoise

2 Tbsp./30 mL butter

1/2 lb./225 g fresh mushrooms, sliced

1/2 lb./225 g shiitake mushrooms, sliced

1/2 lb./225 g oyster mushrooms, sliced

2 Tbsp./30 mL chopped parsley

1 tsp./5 mL chopped thyme

1 beaten egg

Salt and freshly ground black pepper to taste

FOR THE RIESLING SAUCE:

1 medium Spanish onion

1 leek, cleaned

13 oz./375 mL Riesling wine

12 whole black peppercorns

1 bay leaf

1 1/2 cups/360 mL 35% whipping cream

1 recipe Strudel Dough (page 26)

▶ Serves six

Cut the bread into small cubes and put them in a stainless steel bowl with the milk. Heat the butter in a frying pan and sauté the shallots for 3 minutes. Add the mushrooms and continue to sauté for 10 minutes. Keep cooking until most of the liquid from the mushrooms evaporates. Add the parsley and thyme and remove from the heat.

Squeeze excess milk from the soaking bread cubes and add the bread to the mushroom mixture. Add the beaten egg and mix well. Season to taste with salt and pepper.

Slice the onion and leek and place in a saucepan with the Riesling, peppercorns, and

bay leaf. Reduce to a syrupy consistency. In a separate saucepan reduce the cream until it is as thick as paint. Add the cream to the wine reduction. Purée in a food processor and pass through a fine sieve. Reserve.

Preheat an oven to 350°F/175°C. If you are rolling your own strudel, lay an unfancy table-cloth over a card table. Dust the surface with flour. Roll the strudel dough as thinly as you can in the center of the card table. Using fingertips, not fingernails, gently pull the dough towards the edges of the table. When you are finished, you will have created a second "table-cloth" that completely drapes the table. Brush melted butter over the entire surface of the dough. Mound the mushroom filling along one edge of the table as if you were going to make a giant cigarette using the strudel dough as a rolling paper. Cover the mushroom filling with dough and roll the strudel gently towards the opposite end of the table. Tighten and straighten the mixture as you go. When you reach the opposite end, trim any excess dough from the strudel and transfer the strudel to a nonstick baking sheet. Bake for 30 minutes or until the pastry is golden brown.

Presentation:

Lay out six warmed plates. Pour a pool of sauce into the middle of each plate. Slice the strudel diagonally into slices approximately 2 inches/ 5 cm wide. Place a slice on each pool of sauce. Serve at once.

With Anne, Alex, and Ken at Eigensinn at a benefit for prairie farmers in crisis.

Beef Carpaccio with Crispy Brioche

If you live in a town that has a French bakery, purchase a loaf of brioche. If not, a loaf of egg bread will do.

1 lb./455 g beef tenderloin
1 loaf brioche

FOR THE GARNISH:
1 quart/litre jar Pickled Tomato Peppers (page 155)
1 quart/litre jar Pickled Jardinière Vegetables
   (page 112)

Salt and freshly ground black pepper to taste
1 Tbsp./15 mL fresh lemon juice
2 Tbsp./30 mL fine olive oil
1/4 cup/60 mL Parmigiano Reggiano, cut into slivers
2 Tbsp./30 mL roughly chopped Italian parsley

▶Serves six

Trim the beef tenderloin clean of any surface fat. Place in the coldest part of your refrigerator to chill for 3 hours.

Preheat an oven to 275°F/135°C. Slice the bread. Open the oven door and pull out the oven rack. Drape 12 slices of bread over two rungs of the oven rack so that they hang down. Close the oven door and toast until golden and crispy.

Presentation:

Arrange pickled peppers and vegetables in a pleasing pattern on each plate. Place two pieces of crispy brioche in the center of each plate. Use a sharp knife to slice the beef tenderloin as thinly as possible. Drape two or three slices over the brioche on each plate. Season with salt and black pepper and sprinkle with lemon juice. Drizzle with olive oil and sprinkle with Parmesan slivers. Sprinkle with chopped parsley. Serve at once.

Facing page: Beef Carpaccio with Crispy Brioche
   (this page)
Following page: Roasted Vegetable Broth (page 130)

Smoky Tomato Soup

¹/₄ lb./113 g smoked bacon slices

1 Spanish onion, finely diced

2 cloves garlic, finely chopped

2 lbs./900 g roughly chopped ripe tomatoes

10 cups/2 litres Tomato Consommé (page 14)

Salt and freshly ground black pepper to taste

¹/₂ cup/120 mL tomato concassé

6 Tbsp./90 mL sour cream

1 Tbsp./15 mL julienne of basil

▶ Serves six

Roughly chop the bacon slices. Place them in a soup pot over medium heat. Stir until the bacon starts to release some fat. Add the onion and garlic and continue sautéing until the onions start to turn golden. Add the roughly chopped tomatoes. When the mixture starts to boil, add the tomato consommé. Let the soup simmer for 30 minutes. Season with salt and pepper.

Purée the soup in a food processor and strain through a sieve.

Presentation:

Warm six soup bowls. Place some tomato concassé in each bowl. Ladle some soup into each bowl. Place a dollop of sour cream in the center of the soup. Sprinkle with basil julienne. Serve at once.

Facing page: Chestnut Ice Cream with Warm
  Chocolate Sauce (page 154)
Previous page: Roast Galantine of Capon (page 144)

Roasted Vegetable Broth with Arugula Pesto

8 cups/2 litres Tomato Consommé (page 14)

FOR THE GARNISH:

3 Tbsp./45 mL finely diced sweet potato

3 Tbsp./45 mL finely diced leek

3 Tbsp./45 mL tomato brunoise

3 Tbsp./45 mL finely diced zucchini

FOR THE ARUGULA PESTO:

12 leaves arugula, washed

1 clove garlic, finely chopped

2 Tbsp./30 mL shelled walnuts

6 Tbsp./90 mL fine olive oil

3 Tbsp./45 mL grated Parmigiano Reggiano

Salt and freshly ground black pepper to taste

▶Serves six

Prepare the tomato consommé. Preheat an oven to 350°F/175°C. Place all the vegetables, except the tomato, in a cast iron frying pan. Place the pan in the oven and roast, stirring from time to time until the vegetables have shrivelled slightly and browned somewhat. Remove from the oven and reserve.

Roughly chop the arugula leaves and place them in a blender. Add the garlic and walnuts. Turn the blender on and start adding the olive oil in a steady stream. Add the grated Parmesan. Transfer to a bowl and season with salt and pepper.

Presentation:

To serve, heat soup to simmering point. Place some roasted vegetables and some tomato brunoise in each bowl. Place a dollop of pesto in each bowl. Ladle the hot soup into each bowl. Serve at once.

Baked Squash Soup with Sunchoke Purée

2 buttercup squash

4 Tbsp./60 mL butter

1 Tbsp./15 mL finely chopped fresh ginger

1 Tbsp./15 mL finely chopped garlic

Salt and freshly ground black pepper to taste

$^1/_2$ tsp./2.5 mL grated nutmeg

11 cups/2.5 litres Tomato Consommé (page 14)

1 lb./455 g fresh sunchokes (a.k.a. Jerusalem artichokes)

2 Tbsp./30 mL butter

Salt to taste

▶Serves six

Preheat an oven to 350°F/175°C. Split the squash in half and scoop out the seeds. Place the halves flesh side up on a baking sheet. Evenly distribute the butter, ginger, garlic, salt, pepper, and nutmeg into each of the squash cavities. Bake for approximately 1 hour or until the flesh turns soft and yielding. Let the squash sit until it is cool enough to handle. Scoop out the flesh into a soup pot, add 10 cups/2 litres of the consommé and place the pot on medium heat. Simmer the soup for 1 hour.

Carefully peel the sunchokes, roughly cut them into pieces and place them in a small saucepan. Add the remaining consommé and season to taste with salt. Cover and simmer gently for 30 minutes or until the sunchokes are soft. Transfer to a food processor and purée while adding the butter. Season with salt and reserve.

Transfer the squash soup to a food processor and purée in batches. Return the soup to the pot and bring back to the simmering point.

Presentation:

Ladle the soup into six warmed soup bowls. Place a dollop of sunchoke purée in the center of each bowl. Garnish with a small sprig of parsley.

Roasted Red Pepper Soup
with Semolina Dumplings

FOR THE SOUP:

1 Tbsp./15 mL olive oil for cooking

3 cloves garlic, finely chopped

1 Tbsp./15 mL fresh oregano leaves

1 quart/litre jar Roasted Red Peppers (page 155)

8 cups/2 litres Tomato Consommé (page 14)

Salt and freshly ground black pepper to taste

FOR THE DUMPLINGS:

1 cup/240 mL milk

2 eggs

3 Tbsp./45 mL melted butter

1/3 cup/80 mL semolina flour

1/3 cup/80 mL all purpose flour

3 Tbsp./45 mL roughly chopped parsley

1/4 tsp./1.2 mL ground nutmeg

Salt to taste

▶Serves six

Measure the olive oil and garlic into a large soup pot over medium heat. Sauté briefly, but try not to let the garlic brown. Add the roasted red peppers and the oregano leaves and continue to sauté for 5 minutes. Add the consommé and simmer for 30 minutes. Purée the soup, and then return it to a simmer. Adjust seasoning with salt and pepper.

Pour the milk and eggs into a stainless steel bowl and let them come to room temperature. Mix in the melted butter, semolina, and flour. Add the parsley, nutmeg, and salt to taste. Mix well. Bring a large saucepan of salted water to a boil.

Let the dough rest for 30 minutes, then form small round dumplings with a teaspoon and drop them into the water. Simmer the dumplings for 10 minutes. Test for doneness by slicing one in half to see if it is cooked all the way through. Keep the dumplings warm in cooking water.

Presentation:

Place three dumplings in each of six warmed soup bowls. Ladle soup over them. Serve at once.

Lentil Soup with Grilled Sausages

2 cups/480 mL green lentils (preferably French)

2 Tbsp./30 mL butter

2 Spanish onions, finely chopped

2 cloves garlic, finely chopped

3 Tbsp./45 mL Dijon mustard

2 Tbsp./30 mL white wine vinegar

4$^1/_4$ cups/1 litre Chicken Stock (page 14)

4$^1/_4$ cups/1 litre Tomato Consommé (page 14)

2 bay leaves

Salt and freshly ground black pepper to taste

6 Sausages (page 85)

▶Serves six

Soak the lentils in water for 1 hour before use. Melt the butter in a large soup pot and add the onions and garlic. Sauté for 5 minutes, stirring from time to time to prevent browning. Add the soaked lentils, mustard, vinegar, chicken stock, and tomato consommé. Bring to a boil. Add the bay leaves and adjust seasoning. Simmer for 2 hours or until the lentils are soft, almost mushy.

Prepare the sausages and cook them. While still warm, slice them diagonally.

Presentation:

Ladle soup into warmed bowls. Place slices of sausage in the center of each bowl. Serve at once.

Skate with Feta Sautéed Vegetables

Skate is from a type of ray that is popular in Europe and is gaining popularity here. It has an interesting long-grained texture that resembles corduroy. When eaten very fresh it has a wonderful flavor.

FOR THE VEGETABLES:

1 cup/240 mL cooked, sliced new potatoes

2 Tbsp./30 mL olive oil for cooking

1/2 cup/120 mL blanched cauliflower

1/2 cup/120 mL blanched broccoli

1/2 cup/120 mL sliced Roasted Red Peppers (page 155)

1/2 cup/120 mL French or Italian olives

1/4 cup/60 mL tomato concassé

1/4 cup/60 mL sliced green onions

1 Tbsp./15 mL roughly chopped fresh oregano

6 Tbsp./90 mL coarsely crumbled feta

1 clove garlic, finely chopped

Salt and freshly ground black pepper to taste

FOR THE FISH:

3 Tbsp./45 mL olive oil for cooking

6 skinless boneless skate wings

Salt and black pepper

FOR THE SAUCE:

6 Tbsp./90 mL dry red wine

1 Tbsp./15 mL red wine vinegar

2 Tbsp./30 mL butter

▶Serves six

Preheat an oven to 375°F/190°C. Fry the sliced potatoes in olive oil in a large frying pan until crispy on both sides. Add the cauliflower, broccoli, red peppers, and olives. Add the rest of the ingredients and then place the frying pan in the oven. Heat another large frying pan and add the olive oil. When the oil starts to smoke, add the skate fillets. Season with salt and pepper. When the fillets are golden brown on the bottom, turn them over and place the frying pan in the oven. Take the vegetables out when you put the fish in the oven. Leave the fish in the oven for 5 minutes or until the fillets are solid white and the flesh comes apart easily.

Finishing the sauce and presentation:

Set out six warmed dinner plates. Place some of the feta/vegetable mixture on each plate. Drape a cooked fillet over each mound of vegetables. Discard the cooking oil, return the fish pan to high heat, and pour in the red wine and red wine vinegar. Reduce the liquid until it is syrupy and most of the water has evaporated from it. Remove from the heat and whisk in the butter. Spoon a small amount of sauce on each plate. Serve at once.

Piquant Grilled Salmon
with Risotto Filled Peppers

FOR THE PEPPERS:

2 Tbsp./30 mL olive oil for cooking

1¹/₂ cups/360 mL Tomato Consommé (page 14)

2 cloves garlic, split in half

1 small Spanish onion, cut into brunoise

1 cup/240 mL Arborio or other risotto rice

3 Tbsp./45 mL grated Parmigiano Reggiano

1 Tbsp./15 mL chopped parsley

1 Tbsp./15 mL finely chopped chives

6 small cubanelle peppers

FOR THE SALMON:

6 fresh salmon fillets

2 green chilies, finely chopped

Coarse salt

▶Serves six

Heat the oil in a large frying pan. In another pot, warm the consommé. Add the split garlic and the onion to the hot oil. Sauté without browning for 5 minutes. Add the rice and continue to sauté for 5 minutes. Add the consommé little by little, stirring continually, until all the liquid is absorbed by the rice. Stir in the grated cheese and the herbs. Remove from the heat.

Cut the stems from the six peppers and use a paring knife to remove the pith and seeds. Stuff the peppers with the risotto mixture. Place the peppers in a large frying pan with enough tomato consommé to cover the bottom of the pan; cover and reserve.

Preheat an oven to 350°F/175°C. Rub the salmon fillets with the chopped chilies and sprinkle liberally with coarse salt. Five minutes before you plan to start grilling the salmon, place the covered pan of stuffed peppers in the oven. Grill the salmon on the barbeque, approximately 3 minutes per side or to the desired doneness.

Presentation:

Warm six plates. Remove the peppers from the oven after approximately 30 minutes. They should be heated through and the rice should have begun to expand. Slice each pepper and arrange the slices in an overlapping fan pattern, one pepper to a plate. Place a fillet of cooked salmon beside each pepper. Spoon some of the cooking liquid from the pepper pan onto each plate. Serve at once.

Poached Halibut
with Pumpkin Vin Blanc Sauce

FOR THE SAUCE:

2.2 lbs./1 kg halibut or other whitefish bones

1 Spanish onion, sliced

1 fennel bulb, cleaned and sliced

1 small celery root, peeled and sliced

1, 25-oz./750-mL bottle dry white wine

1 cup/240 mL 35% whipping cream

1 cup/240 mL Jamaican pumpkin, roughly chopped

Salt to taste

FOR THE HALIBUT:

$^1\!/_2$ cup/120 mL dry white wine

2 shallots, peeled and cut into brunoise

Freshly ground black pepper to taste

1 Tbsp./15 mL butter

6, 6-oz./170-g fillets fresh halibut

12 new potatoes, cooked and peeled

1 leek, cleaned and cut into brunoise

▶Serves six

Put the bones, onion, fennel, celery root, and white wine into a large saucepan. Simmer for 45 minutes. Transfer to a food processor and purée. Pass through a fine sieve, pour the strained fumet back into the saucepan and continue to simmer.

Pour the cream into a separate saucepan and simmer until it has reduced in volume by two-thirds.

Meanwhile, steam or boil the pumpkin until it is soft. Combine the reduced cream, fumet, and steamed pumpkin in a food processor. Pass through a fine sieve back into the saucepan. Adjust seasoning. Reserve.

Preheat an oven to 350°F/175°C.

Combine the white wine and shallots in an ovenproof baking dish. Season with salt and pepper. Dot with butter. Bring this liquid to the simmering point on the stove. Place the fish fillets in the simmering shallot liquid. Cover with aluminum foil and poach in the oven for 8 minutes.

Boil the potatoes until soft. Boil or steam the leek brunoise until the pieces are tender.

Remove the fish from the oven and pour the poaching liquid into a saucepan. Keep the fish covered with the foil to keep warm. Boil the poaching liquid until it is syrupy, then add the reserved pumpkin sauce.

Presentation:

Warm six plates. Place a cooked fillet on each plate. Ladle sauce over the fillet. Surround the fish with boiled potatoes and sprinkle with leek brunoise. Serve at once.

Muscovy Duck Breast and Confit Leg
with Apples and Crabapple Glaze

1, 3-lb./1.3-kg Muscovy duck

Coarse sea salt

12 whole peppercorns

2 bay leaves

2 sprigs fresh thyme

3 cloves garlic

2 cups/480 mL rendered duck, chicken, or goose fat

2.2 lbs./1 kg crabapples

$^1/_2$ cup/120 mL water

$1^1/_2$ cups/360 mL sugar

2.2 lbs./1 kg Cortland or Mutsu apples

1 cup/240 mL duck jus (see Chicken Jus, page 15)

▶ Serves six

Ask the butcher to bone the duck for you. The legs require a much longer time to cook than the breasts so should be cooked separately. Marinate the legs for 2 hours in a mixture of the salt, peppercorns, bay leaf, thyme, and garlic. After 2 hours melt the rendered fat in a large ovenproof dish with a lid. Preheat an oven to 275°F/135°C. Place the legs and marinade in the fat, cover, and place in the oven for 3 hours. When you remove, the meat should be falling off the bone. Reserve.

Wash and quarter the crabapples. Place them in a saucepan with the water and sugar. Cover and simmer for 30 minutes or until they are mushy like applesauce. Layer cheesecloth over a bowl or use a jelly bag. Transfer the crabapple mixture to the bag and let it hang at room temperature for 12 hours over a small saucepan. Place this saucepan on medium heat and let simmer until syrupy. Peel, quarter, and core the apples. Cut into bite-sized pieces and put in the crabapple reduction. Cover and simmer for 30 minutes or until the pieces are soft but not mushy. Reserve.

Preheat an oven to 400°F/200°C. Season the duck breasts with salt and pepper. Heat an ovenproof frying pan and fry the breasts skin side down until the skin is golden and crispy. Turn briefly so that the flesh side has a chance to sear. Turn back to the skin side and put the pan in the oven. Roast for 8 minutes. Remove from the pan.

Place the legs in the pan and return to the oven to crisp up. After 10 minutes, remove. Keep the duck jus and apples in crabapple glaze at simmering point, separately, for serving.

Presentation:

Warm six plates. Place a small mound of apple mixture with some liquid on each plate. Add some pieces of leg meat to each plate. Carve each breast into nine slices across the grain. Arrange three slices in a fan pattern leaning against the leg/apple mixture. Ladle a pool of jus in front of the breast meat on each plate. Serve at once.

Rosemary Grilled Chicken Breast
with Roasted Pepper Sauce

FOR THE SAUCE:

1 Tbsp./15 mL olive oil for cooking

1 clove garlic, finely chopped

²/₃ cup/160 mL Roasted Red Peppers (page 155),
   roughly chopped

4 Tbsp./60 mL dry white wine

2 cups/480 mL Chicken Jus (page 15)

FOR THE CHICKEN:

6 boneless chicken breasts with skin

Salt and black pepper to taste

6 rosemary branches

▶Serves six

Heat a large saucepan on medium heat. Add
the olive oil, garlic, and roasted red peppers.
Stir continually until the peppers are nicely
browned. Deglaze with the white wine and
reduce until the wine has evaporated. Add the
chicken jus. Simmer for 1 hour. Purée in a
blender and pass through a fine sieve. Reserve.

Prepare the gas or charcoal barbeque.
Season the chicken breasts with salt and black
pepper. Place the branches of fresh rosemary
on the barbeque and top each one with a
chicken breast, skin side down. Grill until
golden brown on the skin side. Turn the breasts
and finish cooking. It usually takes 8 minutes
per side.

Presentation:

Warm six plates. Pour a pool of sauce on each
plate. Place a chicken breast with its rosemary
spear on the sauce. Serve with boiled potatoes
and salad.

Cabbage Roll
with Chanterelle and Tomato Fondue

12 whole leaves of Savoy or green cabbage

FOR THE FILLING:

3 slices of white bread

$^1/_2$ cup/120 mL milk

3 slices smoked bacon, cut into brunoise

3 Tbsp./45 mL Spanish onion, cut into brunoise

1 $^1/_2$ cup/360 mL fresh chanterelles (see page 74)

2 Tbsp./30 mL roughly chopped Italian parsley

1 tsp./5 mL roughly chopped fresh thyme

Salt and freshly ground black pepper to taste

FOR THE SAUCE:

1 cup/240 mL dry red wine

1 quart/litre jar Tomato Sauce (page 156)

1 Tbsp./15 mL butter

FOR THE GARNISH:

6 Tbsp./90 mL sour cream

6 small parsley sprigs

▶ Serves six

Bring a large soup pot of salted water to a boil. Blanch the cabbage leaves one or two leaves at a time until they are pliable, approximately 5 minutes for each batch. Reserve.

Cut the bread into cubes and put them in a bowl with the milk. Sauté the bacon gently in a frying pan with the onion for 5 minutes. Add the chanterelles and continue to sauté for 10 minutes. Add the parsley and thyme. Season with salt and pepper. Transfer the mushroom mixture to a stainless steel mixing bowl. Squeeze the milk from the bread cubes and mix them well with the mushroom mixture. Lay out the blanched cabbage leaves on the counter, facing the same way. Place some filling in each leaf, at the base. Roll the leaves up and fold in the sides so that you have a sealed roll. Place the rolls in a buttered ovenproof baking dish. Preheat an oven to 350°F/175°C.

Pour the red wine into a saucepan. Simmer to reduce its volume by half. Add the tomato sauce. Bring to a simmer and then ladle the sauce over the cabbage rolls. Cover with foil and bake for 30 minutes or until the cabbage is very soft and tender.

Presentation:

Warm six plates. Place a cabbage roll on each plate and ladle a generous amount of sauce over top. Place a dollop of sour cream on each roll. Garnish the cream with a sprig of parsley. Serve at once.

Corn Risotto with Tomato Sauce

FOR THE RICE:

2 Tbsp./30 mL olive oil for cooking

2 cloves garlic, split in half

1 Spanish onion, cut into brunoise

2 cups/480 mL short grained Italian rice
   (e.g., Arborio)

2$^1/_2$ cups/600 mL Tomato Consommé (page 14)

3 cobs of corn, kernels removed (page 122)

$^1/_4$ cup/60 mL dry white wine

$^1/_4$ cup/60 mL 35% cream

$^1/_2$ cup/120 mL grated Parmigiano Reggiano

2 Tbsp./30 mL coarsely chopped fresh sage

FOR THE SAUCE:

1 quart/1 litre Tomato Sauce (page 156)

2 Tbsp./30 mL fine olive oil

▶ Serves six

Pour the olive oil into a large saucepan. Add the garlic and the onion brunoise. Gently sauté for 5 minutes without browning. Add the rice and continue to sauté for 5 minutes. Warm the tomato consommé in a separate saucepan. Ladle the consommé into the rice gradually, stirring continuously over low heat. Add more liquid only as the rice absorbs it. When you have about one quarter of the consommé left, add the corn kernels to the rice. Continue to stir. When the consommé is completely absorbed, add the wine and cream.

When these liquids are almost all absorbed, add the grated Parmigiano Reggiano and the sage.

In a separate saucepan, heat the tomato sauce. When it comes to the boil, stir in the olive oil.

Presentation:

Warm six plates. Place a large dollop of corn risotto on each plate. Ladle some sauce around each mound of risotto. Serve at once.

Grilled Chicken Salad
with Radicchio and Endive

6 shallots, peeled and sliced

3 Tbsp./45 mL white wine vinegar

3 boneless chicken breast

1 tsp./5 mL roughly chopped rosemary leaves

1 green chili, finely chopped

18 green olives, sliced

$^1/_2$ cup/120 mL Emmenthal cheese, cut into julienne

$^1/_2$ cup/120 mL julienne radicchio leaves

4 Tbsp./60 mL fine olive oil

Salt to taste

▶ Serves six

Prepare the gas or charcoal barbeque for grilling. Place the shallots in a stainless steel bowl with the white wine vinegar. Coat the chicken breasts with rosemary and season with salt.

When the grill is hot, start cooking the chicken breasts. They will take approximately 5 minutes on each side. They are done when the breasts are firm to the touch and are opaque through the middle.

When the breasts are cool enough to handle, slice them into thick julienne and mix them with the sliced shallots and vinegar. Add the rest of the ingredients to the bowl and taste for salt.

Serve mounded on plates, with toast.

Bill Hoy making the bread at Superior.

Vegetarian Pot-au-Feu

*E*very culinary tradition
has its version of the
French pot-au-feu; the
German eintopf, the Italian
bollito misto, the Spanish
cocida, or the English boiled
dinner. This recipe is a
vegetarian take on the
French pot-au-feu, which
is often served with horseradish sauce.

FOR THE VEGETABLES:

6 peeled young carrots

6 peeled young parsnips

6 new potatoes

6 2-inch/5-cm lengths of leek, cleaned

6 young white turnips

1 cleaned artichoke, cut into 6 pieces

2 beets

2 cobs corn

$^{1}/_{2}$ cup/120 mL fresh peas

1 sprig of fresh thyme

FOR THE SAUCE:

1 Tbsp./15mL butter

1 Tbsp./15mL all purpose flour

1$^{1}/_{2}$ cups/360 mL milk

1 bay leaf

1 clove

4 Tbsp./60 mL grated horseradish

1 tsp./5 mL white wine vinegar

Salt to taste

FOR THE BOUILLON:

2 cups/480 mL Tomato Consommé (page 14)

Serves six

Prepare all of the vegetables. Keep the carrots
whole or cut in half lengthwise. Keep the potatoes and turnips whole. Cut the corn cobs in
half. Prepare and cook the beets by steaming or
boiling for 45 minutes. Cut into 6 pieces.

Melt the butter in a saucepan. Add the flour.
This will form a sandy paste called a roux. Add
the milk very slowly to the roux while keeping
the heat on low and stirring continuously. Add
the bay leaf and clove. Cook for 30 minutes.
Add the grated horseradish and the vinegar,
then strain the sauce through a fine sieve. Taste
for salt, adjust, and reserve.

Pour the tomato consommé into a large
soup pot. Heat to boiling point and add all
the vegetables except the beets. Simmer for
8 minutes.

Presentation:

Warm six bowls. Distribute the vegetables
evenly among the bowls. Add the beets. Ladle
some consommé into each bowl. Put the sauce
in a sauce-boat. Serve at once.

Herb Crepe with Chanterelles à la Crème

FOR THE CREPE BATTER:

4 eggs

2 cups/480 mL whole milk

Salt to taste

3 Tbsp./45 mL melted butter

3 Tbsp./45 mL finely chopped parsley

$^1/_2$ tsp./2.5 mL coarsely chopped thyme

$^1/_4$ tsp./1.2 mL freshly grated nutmeg

$^3/_4$ cup/180 mL sifted pastry flour

FOR THE CHANTERELLES:

$^1/_2$ cup/120 mL whipped 35% cream

$1^1/_2$ lbs./680 g fresh chanterelles (see page 74)

3 Tbsp./45 mL butter

2 shallots, peeled and finely chopped

$^1/_4$ cup/60 mL dry white wine

1 Tbsp./15 mL chopped parsley

1 tsp./5 mL coarsely chopped thyme

Salt and freshly ground black pepper to taste

▶ Serves six

Bring the eggs and milk to room temperature. Beat them in a stainless steel bowl. Add the salt, melted butter, herbs, and nutmeg. Sift in the flour. Rest the batter for 30 minutes before use.

Use two or more 9-inch/23-cm nonstick frying pans. The number of pans you use at once is directly proportional to your skill as a crepe maker. If you have never done this, I would recommend that you start with one pan.

Place the pan on medium heat. Ladle a thin film of batter into the pan. Do not use any butter. Cook for 1 minute or until the crepe starts to turn golden. Flip the crepe and cook for approximately half the time on the other side. Repeat until all the crepe batter is finished. Unused crepes may be frozen for later use. You will need six crepes for this recipe. Cover the crepes with a damp napkin while you prepare the chanterelle filling.

Whip the cream. Reserve. Dust the chanterelles with a brush or cloth. Place a large frying pan over medium heat. Add the butter and the shallots. After 2 minutes add the chanterelles and sauté. Add the white wine, herbs, and seasoning and sauté for 5 minutes more. The mushrooms will release some liquid and when most of it has evaporated, gently fold in the whipped cream.

Presentation:

Warm six plates. Place a crepe on each plate. Spoon some mushroom mixture in the center of the crepe. Fold the crepe over the mushrooms. Serve at once.

Roast Galantine of Capon
with Mushroom Duxelles and Yukon Gold Mashed Potatoes

FOR THE CAPON:

1, 5-lb./2-kg capon or large chicken

FOR THE JUS:

12 Tbsp./180 mL Chicken or Capon Jus (page 15)

FOR THE DUXELLES:

1 lb./455 g mushrooms

2 shallots, cut into brunoise

$^1/_2$ cup/120 mL white wine

Salt and freshly ground black pepper to taste

FOR THE MASHED POTATOES:

6 Yukon Gold potatoes

2 cups/480 mL milk

4 Tbsp./60 mL butter

Salt to taste

pinch freshly grated nutmeg

FOR THE ONIONS:

1 Spanish onion, cut into 6 wedges

1 red onion, cut into 6 wedges

6 whole green onions

▶Serves six

This part of the recipe, as well as the making of the jus, should be done a day ahead. Ask the butcher to bone the chicken or capon. You may want to bone the capon yourself, but be prepared to spend an hour or more. The idea is to remove all the bones while leaving the bird in one piece so that it may be filled and tied.

After the bird is boned, refrigerate it. Make the jus with the bones (page 15).

The next day, preheat an oven to 275°F/135°C. Brush any dust from the mushrooms, then chop them in a food processor. They should resemble coarse-grained sand. Place the mushrooms on a baking tray. Add the shallot brunoise and the white wine and seasonings and place the tray in the oven. Stir the mushroom mixture from time to time until most of the liquid evaporates and the texture is like moist cake crumbs. Take the tray out of the oven and cool.

When the duxelles are cool, take the boneless capon out of the refrigerator. Lay it on the counter and sprinkle liberally with the duxelles. Reserve 2 Tbsp./60 mL of duxelles for garnishing the plates. Increase the oven temperature to 325°F/165°C. Roll the capon up and tie it with butcher string. Place the tied bird in a roasting pan in the oven and roast for approximately 1 hour, basting the bird occasionally.

While the roast is in the oven, cook the potatoes, unpeeled, in boiling, salted water. In a separate pot, warm the milk and butter.

Check doneness of the roast with a meat thermometer. The interior temperature should be 160°F/ 75°C. Remove the roast from the oven and place it on a rack to cool. Add the onions to the roasting pan and return the pan to the oven.

While the onions are roasting, finish preparing the mashed potatoes. Drain the cooking water from the potato pot. Peel the potatoes, add them to the milk and butter and mash. Taste and adjust for salt and nutmeg. Check doneness of the onions (they should be soft and sweet). The onions will be delicious because they soak up the drippings from the roasting bird as they cook.

Warm the jus in a small saucepan.

Presentation:

Warm six dinner plates. Place a mound of mashed potatoes in the center of each plate. Carve a thick slice of capon and place it on top of the mashed potatoes. Wrap a roasted green onion around the mashed potatoes.

Splay the wedges of red and Spanish onions to make fans and place them separately atop the mashed potatoes. Ladle some jus to the outside of the mashed potatoes. Sprinkle the plate with duxelles. Serve at once.

Roast Entrecôte of Beef with Wild Mushrooms
and Marrow Toasts

FOR THE BEEF:

2 cloves garlic, chopped

1 Tbsp./15 mL roughly chopped fresh thyme

Liberal amounts salt and black pepper

2, 1-lb./455-g steaks, "New York" or "entrecôte"

3 Tbsp./45 mL sunflower oil

FOR THE SAUCE:

1/2 cup/120 mL dry red wine

2 shallots, cut into brunoise

6 cracked black peppercorns

1 cup/240 mL Beef Jus (page 15)

FOR THE TOASTS:

6, 1-inch/2.5-cm pieces of beef marrow bones

6 slices bread, cut into wedges

12 slices beef marrow

Coarse grained sea salt to taste

FOR THE MUSHROOMS:

2 Tbsp./30 mL unsalted butter

1 lb./455 g assortment of wild mushrooms

Salt and freshly ground black pepper to taste

FOR THE GARNISH:

6 sprigs of Italian parsley

▶Serves six

Rub the garlic, thyme, salt, and pepper into the steaks. Reserve.

Pour the wine into a small saucepan with the shallots and the peppercorns. Reduce this until it reaches a syrupy stage. Add the beef jus and reduce to half its volume. Reserve.

Blanch the marrow bones briefly in boiling water to loosen the marrow. Push the marrow out and slice it into 12 pieces.

Preheat an oven to 275°F/135°C. Toast the bread wedges in the oven until golden. Remove the toasts from the oven and arrange two slices of marrow on each toast. Sprinkle with coarse grained salt. Reserve.

Place a large frying pan over medium heat. Melt the butter in the pan and sauté the mushrooms until most of their liquid has evaporated. Season with salt and pepper. Reserve.

Increase the oven temperature to 350°F/175°C. Place a large frying pan with the sunflower oil over high heat. When the oil begins to smoke, carefully place the steaks in the pan. Sear on one side until golden brown. Flip the steaks and place them in the oven. The cooking time depends on how you like your steaks cooked. I like medium rare, which takes about 8 minutes in the oven.

Take the steaks out and transfer them to a cutting board. Heat the marrow toasts on a baking sheet in the oven for 3 minutes (just long enough to melt the marrow slightly and to make it glisten with the salt crystals).

Presentation:

Warm six plates. Place a marrow toast on each plate. Spoon some mushrooms around the marrow toast. Carve three or four slices of beef and arrange them in a fan pattern on each plate. Ladle a small pool of sauce beside the beef and garnish with a parsley sprig. Serve at once.

Jackson, Nile, Micha, and Julia.

Lamb Rack with Fava Bean Risotto

It is possible to buy lamb racks that are "oven ready." This means that the awkward trimming has already been done and that all that remains is to season and roast. The only drawback is that this is usually a frozen product. Sourcing fresh and local produce is part of the joy of cooking seasonally, so find a butcher who carries fresh, local lamb and ask to have it trimmed. Lamb racks usually have seven chops.

FOR THE SAUCE:

5 cloves garlic, unpeeled

1 cup/240 mL Lamb Jus (page 15)

FOR THE LAMB:

3 cloves garlic, finely chopped

1 Tbsp./15 mL coarsely chopped fresh rosemary

2 Tbsp./30 mL Dijon mustard

3 trimmed lamb racks

Salt and freshly ground black pepper to taste

2 Tbsp./30 mL sunflower oil

FOR THE RISOTTO:

1 recipe Corn Risotto (page 140) (subsitute fava beans for corn)

1 cup/240 mL shucked fresh fava beans

▶ Serves six

Preheat an oven to 400°F/200°C. Wrap the 5 cloves of garlic in aluminum foil and place this foil package in the oven. Roast until the heady aroma of roasting garlic hangs heavy in the air. Take the garlic out of the oven. When the cloves are cool enough to handle, peel them and transfer the roasted garlic to a blender. Warm the lamb jus to simmering point.

With the blender running, pour the lamb jus in a steady stream into the blender. This process will flavor and thicken the sauce. Reserve.

Make a paste with the 3 cloves of garlic, rosemary, and Dijon mustard. Season the lamb racks liberally with this paste. Put the racks in a roasting pan, making sure to leave space between them for air to circulate. After

30 minutes, check for doneness by inserting a thermometer into the center of the meat. For medium, the temperature should be 145°F/60°C.

While the lamb racks are roasting, start to make the risotto. Follow the instructions for the Corn Risotto, substituting fava beans for corn.

Remove the lamb from the oven and let it rest for 10 minutes before carving.

Presentation:

Warm six plates. Spoon a mound of risotto onto the center of each plate. Carve the racks of lamb into chops and place three on each plate, with the bones forming a mantle over the risotto. Ladle some sauce around the risotto. Serve at once.

Peach Shortcake with Mascarpone Cream
and Wild Blueberry Compote

FOR THE MASCARPONE CREAM:

3 egg yolks

$^1/_2$ cup/120 mL sugar

Resinous gum from $^1/_2$ vanilla bean

1 cup/240 mL Italian mascarpone

1 cup/240 mL 35% whipping cream

FOR THE SHORTCAKE:

1 cup/240 mL sifted pastry flour

2 tsp./10 mL sugar

1 tsp./5 mL baking powder

$^1/_4$ tsp./1.2 mL baking soda

Pinch salt

$^1/_4$ cup/60 mL cubed butter

$^1/_3$ cup/80 mL buttermilk

FOR THE PEACHES:

1 quart/1 litre Peaches in Vanilla Syrup (page 111)

FOR THE COMPOTE:

1 cup/240 mL Wild Blueberry Compote (page 113)

Icing sugar in a sprinkling can

6 sprigs fresh mint

It is important not to over-mix the shortcake dough in this recipe. It also helps to refrigerate the shortcake rounds before baking.

▶Serves six

Put a soup pot half-filled with water on the stove to boil. Place the egg yolks, sugar, and vanilla in a stainless steel bowl. Reduce the boiling water to a simmer. Whisk the egg yolk/sugar mixture, or sabayon, over the simmering water. Whisk continuously, shifting the bowl periodically away from the heat until the sabayon resembles thick mayonnaise. Remove from heat. Use the whisk to fold in the mascarpone. Blend thoroughly. In a separate bowl whip the cream until soft peaks form. Use a whisk to fold in the whipped cream.

Preheat an oven to 350°F/175°C. Sift the pastry flour, sugar, baking powder, and baking soda together in a stainless steel bowl. Add the salt. Crumble the butter cubes with the dry ingredients. Add the buttermilk all at once and mix together to make a soft dough. Roll out to a thickness of $^3/_4$ inch/1.9 cm and cut out 3-inch/7.5-cm rounds. Bake for 15 minutes.

Presentation:

As soon as the shortcakes are ready, take them out of the oven and split them. Place the bottom half of each shortcake in the center of each plate. Spoon some cream on the bottom halves. Place a peach-half on the cream. Spoon more cream on the peach half. Spoon an overflowing amount of blueberry compote on the cream. Finish with the top half of the shortcake. Dust with icing sugar. Garnish each plate with a sprig of fresh mint. Serve at once.

Poppy Seed Strudel with Poached Plums

It is absolutely vital to the success of this recipe to use ground poppy seeds. If you don't, the filling will not bind, nor will there be any significant release of poppy flavor. I buy my poppy seeds from a Romanian woman in Kensington market, who also has a poppy seed mill. She grinds them fresh for me when I buy them. Once they are ground, it is also important to use them right away because they turn rancid rather quickly.

FOR THE PLUMS:

You can follow the directions for Apricots in Vanilla Syrup (page 111). Substitute greengage or prune plums for the apricots.

1 recipe Strudel Dough (page 26)
$^1/_2$ cup/120 mL melted butter

FOR THE STRUDEL FILLING:

2 cups/480 mL ground poppy seeds
$^1/_2$ cup/120 mL raisins
Zest of 1 lemon
$1^1/_2$ cups/360 mL milk
4 Tbsp./60 mL honey

Icing sugar in a sprinkling can

▶ **Serves six**

Make the strudel dough. While the dough is resting, prepare the poppy seed filling.

Place all the ingredients for the filling in a saucepan. Simmer for 1 hour, stirring from time to time. The seeds will soak up most of the milk and will develop almost a paste consistency. Let the mixture cool at room temperature.

Pull out the strudel dough and paint it with melted butter. Follow the procedure for rolling the strudel on page 126.

Preheat an oven to 350°F/175°C. Bake the strudel for 30 minutes or until golden brown. Remove from the oven and cool to room temperature.

Presentation:

Arrange three plum halves on each plate. Spoon juice over each plum. Slice the strudel on the bias. Place strudel beside the poached plums. Sprinkle icing sugar on each slice of strudel. Serve at once.

Baked Pear Tart with Caramel Sauce

FOR THE TART CRUST:
1 lb./455 g Sweet Pastry (page 24)

1 cup/240 mL sifted pastry flour
$^1/_2$ cup/120 mL melted butter

FOR THE FILLING:
6 firm, ripe Bartlett pears
4 eggs
$^3/_4$ cup/180 mL sugar

FOR THE SAUCE:
1 cup/240 mL sugar
$^1/_2$ cup/120 mL water
2 Tbsp./30 mL butter
6 Tbsp./90 mL 35% whipping cream

▶ Serves six

Select a 10-inch/25-cm scalloped tart form with a removable bottom. Roll out the sweet pastry to a $^1/_4$-inch/.6-cm thickness. Roll the paste up onto the rolling pin and drape it loosely over the tart form. Carefully fit the paste into all the nooks and crannies of the form. Trim the paste, leaving a $^1/_2$-inch/1.2-cm overhang. Preheat an oven to 350°F/175°C.

Fill the tart form with baking beans and blind bake the tart shell for 30 minutes or until golden brown. Remove, but leave the oven on. Peel the pears and slice them thinly. Arrange them in the tart shell in an overlapping circular pattern. Reserve.

Heat a saucepan half-filled with water to the boil. Reduce the heat to a simmer. Crack the eggs into a stainless steel bowl and add the sugar. Whisk the eggs and sugar over the simmering water until they are frothy and have warmed to body temperature. Check the temperature by feeling the side of the bowl with your hand; it should not feel cold or warm. Transfer the mixture to an electric mixer and whisk at high speed until it has tripled in volume. Fold in the pastry flour and the butter. Pour this mixture over the pears in the tart shell. Bake until the filling is golden brown and a skewer inserted in the center comes out clean. Let the tart cool to room temperature.

While the tart is baking, prepare the sauce. Boil the sugar and water in a stainless steel pot. Boil, without stirring, on high heat until the sugar turns amber and begins to smell like caramel. Turn off the heat and add the butter and cream. Be extremely careful when using caramel as the high temperature can cause terrible burns.

Presentation:

Put a wedge of tart on each plate. Spoon some sauce beside each wedge and serve.

Autumn Fruit Soup with Apple Sorbet

Here, I am taking a cooking method normally reserved for warm, savoury consommés and using it for a chilled fruit dessert. The "Parisienne scoops" referred to in the ingredient list are produced by using a "Parisienne knife," also known as a melon baller.

FOR THE SOUP:

1 lb./455 g Northern Spy apples

1/2 lb./225 g Bartlett pears

1/2 lb./225 g black Concord grapes

6 egg whites

1 quart/1 litre white grape juice

FOR THE SORBET:

2 lbs./1 kg Granny Smith apples

1/2 cup/120 mL white grape juice

6 Tbsp./90 mL sugar

FOR THE SOUP GARNISH:

18 whole white Concord grapes

18 whole black Concord grapes

18 Parisienne scoops of unpeeled red Delicious apple

18 Parisienne scoops of unpeeled Bartlett pear

▶ Serves six

Wash the fruit for the soup. Do not peel or take the seeds out. Roughly chop all the fruit and transfer to a soup pot. Add the egg whites and mix very well. Add the white grape juice. Place on the stove to simmer. Stir often while the soup is coming up to the boil.

A raft will form as for consommé. When the raft has formed, stop stirring and cover the pot. Continue to simmer with the lid on for 15 minutes. Strain through a cheesecloth. Chill.

Wash the apples and cut them up roughly. Do not peel or core them. Process them in a blender using the white grape juice to help purée. Pass the purée through a fine sieve. Add the sugar and mix well. Transfer to an ice cream maker and process into sorbet.

Mix all the garnish fruit together and refrigerate.

Presentation:

Chill six soup plates. Divide the fruit among the bowls. Place one scoop of Granny Smith sorbet in the center of each bowl. Ladle soup halfway up the sorbet. The amount of soup is important because the sorbet shouldn't float. Serve at once.

Caramelized Pear Tart
with Rich Chocolate Ice Cream

1 lb./455 g Sweet Pastry (page 24)

1 recipe Crème Anglaise (page 19)

1 1/2 cups/360 mL grated unsweetened chocolate

6 firm, ripe Bartlett pears

Vanilla Syrup (page 111)

Caramel Sauce (page 102)

▶ Serves six

Roll the sweet pastry out to a 1/4-inch/.6-cm thickness. Using a plate with a 7-inch/18-cm diameter as a cutting guide, trace around the plate with a paring knife, cutting through the pastry to form six discs of sweet pastry. Refrigerate the discs.

Make the crème anglaise and, while the mixture is still warm, mix in the grated chocolate. When the chocolate crème anglaise has cooled to room temperature, transfer it to an ice cream maker and process.

Carefully peel the pears using a sharp paring knife. Try to leave the stems attached. Use a melon baller to scoop out the cores by boring through the bottom. Place the pears in the vanilla syrup in a stainless steel saucepan and gently poach them, covered, for 30 minutes or until they are soft to the touch, but not falling apart.

Cool the pears in the syrup to room temperature. When they are cool, slice through each pear several times, leaving the stem end unsliced. When you push down on it, it should fan itself out flat but remain in one piece.

Preheat an oven to 375°F/190°C. Place two 7-inch/18-cm nonstick, ovenproof frying pans on medium heat. Heat 2 Tbsp./30 mL of caramel in each pan. Place a fanned pear in the bubbling caramel. Place a disc of pastry on each pear. Bake for 20 minutes or until the pastry is golden brown.

Now the tricky part; holding a serving plate in one hand and the pan in the other, invert the tart onto the plate.

Repeat this operation until you have six plates with pear tarts.

Presentation:

Return the six plates with the tarts on them to the oven to warm briefly. When you are ready to serve them, place a large dollop of ice cream in the center of each tart. Serve at once.

I once taught this dessert to to a class in Calgary. My teaching assistant, Dee Hobsbawn-Smith, was charged with the responsibility of producing 60 of these tarts in 4 hours. She succeeded with flying colors, so don't be too discouraged if this recipe sounds daunting.

Chestnut Ice Cream
with Warm Chocolate Sauce

1 lb./455 g fresh chestnuts

4 cups/960 mL homogenized milk

4 Tbsp./60 mL honey

1 recipe Crème Anglaise (page 19)

1 recipe Vanilla Wafer Batter (page 25)

1 cup/240 mL grated semisweet chocolate

As with many of my recipes, the amount of effort exerted is directly proportional to excellence of the result. Ideally, the amount of time spent on a recipe should not be important. Roasting and peeling fresh chestnuts is an arduous task, but the result is well worth the trouble. Store the chestnuts in salt water to plump them up a bit, making them a little easier to peel after roasting. I learned this from the chestnut vendor who sets up outside the Royal Ontario Museum.

▶Serves six

One day before you serve this dessert, half fill a soup pot with salty water. Score the shell of the chestnuts with a paring knife. Place the scored chestnuts in the salt water and refrigerate overnight.

The next day, preheat an oven to 375°F/190°C. Place the chestnuts on a baking sheet scored side up. Roast them for 15 minutes or until they split.

Remove the chestnuts and, while they are still warm, peel them. Place the peeled chestnuts with 2 cups/480 mL of the milk, and the honey, in a saucepan. Simmer for 30 minutes.

Purée the chestnut mixture in a blender. Reserve. Place the chestnut purée in a stainless steel bowl. Use a whisk to gradually and smoothly mix in the crème anglaise. Transfer to an ice cream maker and process. Reserve in the freezer.

Grease a baking sheet and spread the wafer batter on it in 3-inch/7.5-cm rounds, spaced 1 inch/2.5 cm apart. Bake them for 8 minutes or until they are golden brown around the edges. Remove the tray from the oven and, while the wafers are still hot, form them into cones. Make sure the bottoms are closed. The cones will set in their shape as they cool.

Place grated chocolate in a stainless steel bowl. Scald 2 cups/480 mL of the milk in a saucepan. Add the milk gradually to the chocolate to melt it. Keep adding the milk until a smooth sauce consistency is obtained. Keep the sauce warm.

Presentation:

Chill six soup bowls. Place three oval scoops of ice cream in each bowl so that they touch in the center, like a trillium. Imbed a cone upright at the point where the three scoops converge. Pour some chocolate sauce into each cone. Serve at once.

Roasted Red Peppers

8 cups/2 litres Tomato Consommé (page 14)
3 cups/720 mL white wine vinegar
3 cloves garlic, sliced

1 Tbsp./15 mL whole black peppercorns
Salt to taste
1 bushel/12 kg sweet red peppers

To prepare the preserving brine, simmer the consommé, vinegar, garlic, and peppercorns. Taste for salt. Reserve.

Light the barbeque. Gas is fine, but hardwood charcoal is the best. When the coals are hot enough to char the skins of the peppers, line the grill with as many peppers as will fit at one time. Char the skin on all sides. As they are roasted, transfer them to a plastic pail with a lid, to steam and cool. Keep the fire stoked and keep roasting until all the peppers are done.

When the peppers are cool enough to handle, peel them and remove the seeds and stems. Sterilize 1-quart/1-litre preserving jars according to package directions. Pack the peppers into the jars.

Pour brine in each jar up to the neck. Place a seal and crown on top and process the jars, submerged in boiling water, for 15 minutes. Remove the jars and let them cool to room temperature. Store in a cool, dark place.

In the fall, excellent peppers are plentiful and inexpensive. We take advantage of this and preserve several bushels. It's fun to get outside before it's too cold and stand at the warmth of a barbeque with the smoky sweet aroma of roasting peppers in the air. Preserved roasted peppers are versatile and appear on my menus throughout the year.

Pickled Tomato Peppers

1 bushel/12 kg tomato peppers
Brine mixture from Roasted Red Peppers (above)

1/2 cup/120 mL sugar

Sterilize jars and prepare seals according to the directions on the package.

Wash the peppers well. Discard any bruised or rotting ones. Split them in half lengthwise and pack them tightly into sterilized jars. Add the sugar to the brine and fill the jars with the brine up to the necks. Place a seal and crown on each jar and process by submerging the jars in boiling water for 15 minutes. Remove the jars and let them cool to room temperature. Store in a cool, dark place.

Tomato peppers are great for preserving because they are thick-fleshed and, when allowed to mature in the jar, become slightly piquant. They are great with antipasti and as a salad ingredient.

Tomato Sauce

The first time I made tomato sauce from scratch I really hadn't done my homework. I knew nothing of the lore and pride that surrounds the endeavor. I hadn't yet cycled down the back alleys of residential neighborhoods in tomato season and caught vignettes of people in their garages, sitting on chairs, hunched over their work, surrounded by ripe tomatoes on tarpaulins stretched over the floor. In fact, my first tomato sauce didn't even look right. It wasn't red. It was orange. A woman in my midst named Potoula, who knew of the lore, looked at my sauce and laughed. Over the years I have continued to make tomato sauce. I know I must be on the right track because the sauce is now a beautiful, deep red.

1 bushel/12 kg Roma tomatoes
20 cloves garlic, sliced

100 fresh basil leaves, coarsely chopped
Salt and freshly ground black pepper to taste

Tomatoes ripen best in the dark. They like to be covered in a blanket or tarp. They like to be at room temperature. Select only sound tomatoes and lay them out wherever you have some space to spare. Cover them and inspect them daily. When they are really red and are beginning to soften, that is the time to make sauce.

Sterilize jars and prepare seals according to the directions on the package.

Wash the tomatoes and chop them coarsely. Put them through a food mill, or a hand-cranked or electric machine that is designed for this purpose.

Place the resulting pulp in a stainless steel pot. Bring it to a boil and add the garlic, basil, and seasonings. Boil for 15 minutes, skimming from time to time. Transfer to jars. Place a seal and crown on each jar. To process, submerge the jars in boiling water for 15 minutes. Remove the jars and cool to room temperature. Store in a cool, dark place.

Marinated Eggplant

1 bushel/12 kg eggplants
Sea salt
6 cups/1.5 litres fine olive oil

2 cups/480 mL white wine vinegar
10 cloves garlic, finely sliced

Poke holes in the bottom of a 5-gallon/20-litre vegetable oil bucket. Place a round perforated pizza pan in the bottom of the bucket. Slice the eggplant into $\frac{1}{8}$-inch/.3-cm rounds. Salt the rounds liberally on both sides and place them on the pizza pan in the bottom of the bucket. You may have to use two buckets. Place a plate that fits snugly inside the bucket on top of the eggplant slices. Place three bricks on top of the plate to weigh the eggplant down. Leave the whole issue over a drain in your sink for two days.

After two days, remove the bricks and plate and rinse the eggplant slices under cool water, squeezing them out to remove the salt. Sterilize jars and prepare seals according to the directions on the package. Pack the slices into sterilized jars.

Mix the oil, vinegar, and garlic. Pour this mixture into the jars up to their necks. Place a seal and crown on each jar. Submerge the jars in boiling water and process for 20 minutes. Remove the jars and cool to room temperature. Store in a cool, dark place.

There are so many kinds of eggplant out there. I have been fortunate to have used several different varieties and the ones I favor for this preserve are the light purple ones, called violet eggplants. They are close to the same shape as conventional eggplant but are about half the size. I find that they are firmer and stand up well to being marinated and preserved.

Our house bread.

Winter

Alex and Anne at the JK ROM booth at "Taste 2000."

Curried Vegetables in Wild Rice Roti

In my company there are people from all over the world. One day we were discussing roti and I learned from Rajes that "roti" actually translates as bread. Making roti is a process of incorporating fat into dough, not totally unlike making puff pastry. I suggested adding some ground wild rice because at that time I had been experimenting with it as an addition to regular wheat flour in pasta and bread recipes. Ground wild rice adds a certain earthy sweetness to breads. The result was delicious. Thanks to our cross-cultural co-operative effort we created something new and delicious.

FOR THE ROTI:

1 1/2 cups/360 mL hard white flour (see Note)

1/2 cup/120 mL finely ground wild rice (see Note)

3/4 cup/180 mL water

Salt to taste

2 Tbsp./30 mL clarified butter plus 1/2 cup/120 mL (page 163)

FOR THE CURRY PASTE:

2 Tbsp./30 mL whole cumin seeds

2 Tbsp./30 mL whole coriander seeds

1 tsp./5 mL whole fenugreek

1/4 tsp./1.2 mL whole fennel seed

2 tsp./10 mL fresh green chilies, finely chopped, including seeds

2 tsp./10 mL ground turmeric

1/2 tsp./2.5 mL freshly chopped ginger

1/2 tsp./2.5 mL freshly chopped garlic

1/4 tsp./1.2 mL freshly ground cinnamon

FOR THE VEGETABLES:

2 medium potatoes

2 bunches fresh spinach leaves

1 cup/240 mL Tomato Sauce (page 156)

2 Tbsp./30 mL curry paste

1/2 cup/120 mL fresh green peas

Salt to taste

FOR THE RAITA:

1 cup/240 mL yogourt

1 grated cucumber

1 Tbsp./15 mL finely sliced mint

2 Tbsp./30 mL clarified butter (page 163)

Salt to taste

▶Serves six

Mix the flours together in a stainless steel bowl. Add the water, salt, and 2 Tbsp./30 mL clarified butter. Knead the dough for 10 minutes. It should have the same consistency as bread dough. Let it rest for 15 minutes, then roll it out as thinly as you can in a circle. Paint the surface of the rolled dough with 1/2 cup/ 120 mL clarified butter. Roll the dough as for strudel (page 126). Now, roll it into a coil. Let the dough rest for a further 30 minutes.

Heat the cumin, coriander, fenugreek and fennel seed in a frying pan. Stir constantly. As the spices heat up they will begin to release their rich aroma. Continue to stir for 5 minutes or until the spices are lightly toasted. Add the remaining curry paste ingredients and continue to stir for an additional 2 minutes. Work the spices into a paste using a mortar and pestle, an electric spice grinder, or a blender. Store paste in a zip lock bag or glass jar with a lid.

Boil the potatoes in their skins until tender. Peel and cut into small dice. Wash the spinach leaves in two changes of water. Dry in a salad spinner. Warm the tomato sauce in a saucepan with the curry paste and bring to a boil. Simmer to evaporate the sauce. Add the spinach and green peas. Continue to cook until most of the liquid has evaporated. Add salt to taste and reserve.

To make raita, mix the yogourt, grated cucumber, and mint in a stainless steel bowl. Transfer to a strainer lined with cheesecloth and suspended over a bowl. Let the yogourt mixture hang in this way until the whey has dripped away. This usually takes 1 hour.

Roll the dough out on the counter or marble slab to $1/8$-inch/.3-cm thickness.

Use a 3-inch/7.5-cm plain round cookie cutter to cut 12 rounds of dough. Place 1 Tbsp./15 mL of filling in each round. Dab a little water along one edge. Bring the edges of the dough together to make crescent-shaped packages.

Place a frying pan on low-medium heat. Add 2 Tbsp./30 mL clarified butter. Fry the rotis slowly until golden on both sides.

Presentation:

Season the raita with salt and place a small bowl in the center of a serving platter. Arrange the fried rotis around the bowl on the platter. Serve as hors d'oeuvres.

Hard flour refers to flour used to make bread. It has a high gluten content which is essential for bread doughs in general and for yeast-raised doughs in particular.

Use a coffee grinder to mill the wild rice to a fine powder similar in texture to semolina flour. If you are fortunate enough to possess a flour mill then use that.

Rajes and Rochelle at Taste.

Tamarind Beef Skewers

1 shallot, peeled and cut into brunoise

1 clove garlic, finely chopped

¼ cup/60 mL tamarind paste

2 Tbsp./30 mL soy sauce

1 Tbsp./15 mL fresh lime juice

1 lb./455 g beef tenderloin

12 skewers

▶ Serves six

Mix all the marinade ingredients together in a stainless steel bowl. Cut the beef into 12 strips, 2 inches/5 cm long. Thread these pieces onto 12 skewers and place them so that they lie flat on a baking sheet. Spoon some marinade over each skewer. Marinate for 1 hour.

Grill the skewers on the barbeque, or on a griddle, for 1 minute on each side or according to your preference.

Arrange skewers on a serving platter and pass as hors d'oeuvres.

Crunchy Shallot "Strudel"

$^1/_2$ cup/120 mL Crème Fraîche (page 19)
1 recipe Crepe Batter (page 20)

6 shallots, peeled and sliced
2 Tbsp./30 mL clarified butter

▶Serves six

Prepare the crème fraîche two days before use. Prepare the crepe batter at least 1 hour before making the crepes. You will need six crepes for this recipe. Prepare the crepes and reserve, covered, at room temperature.

To make clarified butter, simmer the butter gently until all the liquid separates from the melted butter by evaporation. Skim from time to time. Strain through a fine sieve.

Gently sauté the shallots in the clarified butter until they are golden brown. Transfer them to paper towels to drain and crisp. Lay the crepes out on a work surface. Spread a thin layer of crème fraîche on the crepes and sprinkle the surface with the crispy shallots. Roll up the crepes as tightly as you can. Refrigerate them for 1 hour.

Presentation:

Slice the crepe strudels into 1-inch/2.5-cm rounds. Arrange them on a serving platter and pass them as hors d'oeuvres.

Crisp Fried Onions and Parsley

This recipe is a nice bar snack, like salt peanuts, good with beer, to have in the kitchen while preparing dinner. They also make a nice accompaniment to Grilled Steak (page 58).

2 Spanish or Vidalia onions
¼ cup/60 mL milk
¼ cup/60 mL Italian parsley

3 cups/720 mL sunflower oil
1 cup/240 mL all purpose flour for dredging
Salt to taste

▶ Serves six

Peel the onions and slice them into rings as finely as possible. Transfer them to a bowl with the milk and marinate them for 1 hour. Wash the parsley and pat dry with towels.

Heat the oil in a large soup pot to 350°F/175°C. Dredge the onion rings in flour. Shake off the excess flour and fry them in the oil. Move the onions around in the oil with a slotted spoon until golden brown. Lift them out and dry them on paper towels. Sprinkle with salt. Repeat with the parsley.

Presentation:

Place the fried onions on a serving platter. Place the fried parsley on the onions. Serve at once.

At Margaret's lobster boil.

Duck Leg and Crackling Salad
with Lentil Vinaigrette

FOR THE DUCK LEG:
3 Confit duck legs (page 137)

FOR THE VINAIGRETTE:
1/4 cup/60 mL French lentils
1 egg yolk
1 tsp./5 mL Dijon mustard
1 tsp./5 mL white wine vinegar
1 tsp./5 mL lemon juice

3 Tbsp./45 mL sunflower oil
Salt and freshly ground black pepper to taste

FOR THE SALAD:
1 head Belgian endive
1 head frisée (curly endive)
1/2 head escarole
3 bunches lamb's lettuce

In the south of France, duck is traditionally prepared in the early winter to preserve it for use during the winter months. Confit of duck requires cooking the duck legs slowly in rendered duck fat. The legs are then stored in the congealed fat in a cool place and used as required.

▶ Serves six

Prepare the confit duck legs at least a day ahead of time.

Separate the skin from the meat.

Preheat an oven to 350°F/175°C. Place 1 Tbsp./15 mL of the rendered duck fat in a frying pan. Roughly slice the skin into pieces.

Transfer the pieces to the frying pan. Place the frying pan in the oven and crisp the skin until it is golden brown. Transfer the crisped skin to a paper towel to drain. Salt and reserve. This is the crackling. Shred the meat with your fingers. Reserve.

Cook the lentils in salted water for 40 minutes or until they are soft, almost mushy. Drain the water from the cooked lentils. Place the egg yolk in a stainless steel bowl with the mustard,

vinegar, and lemon juice and whisk together. While whisking, pour in the sunflower oil in a thin steady stream. Season with salt and pepper. Add the cooked lentils.

Break the endive, frisée, and escarole into small pieces before washing and spinning. Wash the lamb's lettuce in small clumps.

Toss the salad ingredients without any dressing. Sauté the shredded duck in a frying pan until thoroughly hot. Add the duck to the salad and toss gently.

Presentation:

Place an equal amount of mixed salad on each plate. Spoon the dressing on and around the salad. Place some crackling on each salad. Serve at once.

Endive Salad with Croûtons

This is a salad that is served with a warm dressing. You can really only make this kind of salad using winter lettuces because they are hardy enough to take the heat without wilting.

FOR THE CROÛTONS:

6 slices white bread, crusts removed

3 Tbsp./45 mL rendered duck fat

18 lardons of smoked side bacon

FOR THE SALAD:

1 head Belgian endive

1 head frisée (curly endive)

1 head radicchio

6 Pickled Tomato Pepper halves (page 155)

FOR THE DRESSING:

3 Tbsp./45 mL olive oil for cooking

1 shallot, peeled and finely sliced

1 clove garlic, finely chopped

1 Tbsp./15 mL sherry vinegar

1 tsp./5 mL lemon juice

Salt and freshly ground black pepper to taste

▶ Serves six

Preheat an oven to 275°F/135°C. Place the bread, duck fat, and bacon lardons on the tray. Place the tray in the oven to slowly toast the bread slices until they are golden on both sides.

Meanwhile, the bacon should be getting crisp. Remove the bacon lardons and transfer them to paper towels to drain.

Break all the lettuces into small pieces before washing and spinning dry.

Heat the cooking olive oil in a frying pan. Add the shallots and garlic and sauté over medium heat until the garlic starts to change color. Add the vinegar and lemon juice and remove from heat. Season.

Presentation:

Place a slice of toasted bread on each plate. Put all the lettuces and the pickled peppers in a salad bowl, add the dressing while it is still warm, and toss. Place an equal amount of salad on each of the six croûtons. Sprinkle with the crisp lardons. Serve at once.

Warm Foie Gras with Chestnut
and Black Currant

FOR THE CREPE BATTER:

Follow the directions for Crepe Batter (page 20),
except before adding the flour, mix in:
4 Tbsp./60 mL Chestnut Purée (page 154)

FOR THE FOIE GRAS:

1 lb./455 g fresh foie gras

3 Tbsp./45 mL cognac
Salt to taste

FOR THE BLACK CURRANT PURÉE:

3 Tbsp./45 mL Black Currant Purée (page 114)

▶ Serves six

Prepare the crepe batter, allowing 2 hours
before making the crepes. Take the foie gras out
of the refrigerator and allow it to come to room
temperature. Carefully remove the large veins
and macerate the liver in a stainless steel bowl
with the cognac and salt.

Prepare the crepes. You will need six crepes
for this recipe. The rest you may freeze for
future use. Lay the crepes out on a working
surface. Divide the macerated foie gras into six
equal pieces and place one piece on each
crepe. Wrap the crepes around the foie gras to
form a package.

Preheat an oven to 350°F/175°C. Place the
crepe packages on a baking sheet in the oven.
While the crepes are warming, place the black
currant purée in a saucepan to warm.

When the crepes are soft to the touch and
they start releasing their rich fragrance and
their fat, take them out of the oven.

Presentation:

Warm six plates. Place a small pool of black
currant purée on each plate. Use a spatula to
place one crepe package on each pool of purée.
Spoon some of the rendered fat from the baking
sheet back onto the crepes. Serve at once.

Stilton, Pear, and Rösti Melt

Stilton and pears make one of those undeniably delicious combinations, like tomatoes and basil. In this recipe the addition of warmth and textural counterpoint, in the form of the rösti, takes this good marriage to new heights. This is a wonderful brunch idea. Try it with a glass of port.

6 Rösti (page 73)
3 ripe Bartlett pears

³/₄ lb./340 g Stilton cheese

▶ Serves six

Prepare the rösti and put them on a baking sheet. Preheat an oven to 350°F/175°C. Peel the pears and quarter them. Use a paring knife to scoop out the core. Cut each quarter lengthwise into thirds. Cut the Stilton into similar-sized pieces. Place an equal amount of pear and Stilton onto each rösti. Keeping the rösti on the baking sheet, fold each rösti over the Stilton and pear to form a crescent shaped package. Place the tray with the filled rösti in the oven. Warm until the cheese melts. Use a spatula to transfer the rösti onto six plates. Serve at once.

Tourtière Strudel
with Pickled Jardinière Vegetables

FOR THE FILLING:

2 Tbsp./30 mL butter

1 Spanish onion, finely diced

2 cloves garlic, finely chopped

1/2 lb./227 g ground pork

1/2 lb./227 g ground beef

2 eggs

1 cooked potato, cut into brunoise

1/4 tsp./1.2 mL roughly chopped sage

1/8 tsp./.6 mL ground clove

Salt and freshly ground black pepper to taste

FOR THE STRUDEL:

1 recipe Strudel Dough (page 26)

1/2 cup/120 mL melted butter

FOR THE GARNISH:

1 cup/240 mL Pickled Jardinière Vegetables
   (page 112)

2 Tbsp./30 mL roughly chopped Italian parsley

This recipe can be served as an hors d'oeuvre by itself or plated with jardinière vegetables. The idea for this recipe blends at least two culinary traditions. The Québécois make a meat pie called tourtière. Several eastern European countries share the tradition of savoury or sweet strudels. Here, I have used the strudel dough and filled it with tourtière filling.

▶ Serves six

Melt the butter in a large frying pan on medium heat. Add the onion and garlic. Stir, then add the ground pork and beef.

Sauté for 5 minutes. Transfer to a stainless steel mixing bowl. Add the eggs and the potato brunoise. Mix in the sage, the ground clove, and the seasonings. Mix well and refrigerate.

Pull the strudel dough as on page 126. Paint melted butter over the entire surface of the dough with a pastry brush. Place the filling along one edge of the dough. Roll. Paint melted butter on the finished strudel.

Preheat an oven to 350°F/175°C. Bake the strudel until golden brown.

Presentation:

If you are serving the strudel as an hors d'oeuvre, simply slice it straight across into bite-sized pieces and present it on a serving platter, garnished with some pieces of jardinière vegetables. Otherwise, you could serve this dish as a first course. Slice a larger piece of strudel for each plate. Garnish each plate with a mound of jardinière vegetables. Sprinkle with parsley. Serve at once.

Chicken Consommé
with Ginger and Green Onion

FOR THE CLARIFICATION:

6 boneless chicken legs

1 Spanish onion, roughly chopped

1 carrot, washed and roughly chopped

2 celery stalks, washed and roughly chopped

1 leek, washed and roughly chopped

2 cloves garlic, sliced

6 egg whites

1 small sprig fresh thyme

1 bay leaf

12 whole black peppercorns

Salt to taste

$^1/_4$ tsp./1.2 mL ground nutmeg

12 cups/3 litres Chicken Stock (page 14)

FOR THE GARNISH:

1 green onion

1 Tbsp./15 mL fine julienne of fresh ginger

3 oz./90 mL chicken breast meat

▶Serves six

Combine all the ingredients for the clarification, except the chicken stock, in a large, heavy-bottomed soup pot. It is important to mix the egg whites thoroughly into the clarification before adding the chicken stock. Add the chicken stock and place the pot on low heat. Stir from time to time until the mixture begins to coagulate and form a raft on the surface. The soup should boil gently to allow the stock to percolate through the raft to extract flavor and to clarify. Let the consommé percolate for 2 hours.

Strain the consommé gently through a sieve lined with cheesecloth. Reserve.

Clean the green onion and slice it on the bias as finely as possible. When slicing the fine julienne of fresh ginger, make sure the pieces are no wider than the width of your soup spoon. Cut the breast meat into six equal pieces. Pound the breast meat pieces between two sheets of plastic with a meat pounder or the heel of a saucepan.

Presentation:

Warm six soup bowls. Place an equal amount of green onion and ginger in each bowl. Drape a slice of chicken breast on top. Ladle gently boiling consommé into each bowl. Serve at once.

Curried Vegetable Marrow Soup with Clams

FOR THE SOUP:

1 Spanish onion, cut into brunoise

2 cloves garlic, finely chopped

2 Tbsp./30 mL butter

3 Tbsp./45 mL Curry Paste (page 160)

3 cups/720 mL coarsely chopped vegetable marrow

8 cups/2.5 litres Chicken Stock (page 14)

Salt to taste

FOR THE CLAMS:

1 clove garlic, finely chopped

2 shallots, peeled and cut into brunoise

1 Tbsp./15 mL butter

30 washed littleneck or Manilla clams

4 Tbsp./60 mL dry white wine

FOR THE GARNISH:

6 sprigs fresh cilantro

If no vegetable marrow is to be found, substitute any kind of squash that you can find. Pumpkin also works well.

▶ Serves six

Gently sauté the onion and garlic in the butter in a large saucepan over medium heat for 5 minutes. Add the curry paste and continue to sauté for 2 minutes. Add the vegetable marrow and continue to sauté for 5 minutes. Add the chicken stock and simmer for 20 minutes or until the vegetable marrow is tender.

Transfer the soup to a food processor and purée. Pass through a sieve into another soup pot. Keep at simmering point.

Sauté the garlic and shallots in the butter. After 2 minutes, add the washed clams. Add the white wine and cover the pot. The clams should open after 5 minutes. Discard any that don't.

Put five clams in each of six soup bowls. Arrange the clams in a pleasing pattern with the open side of the shells facing up. Pour the cooking liquid from the clams into the soup. Bring the soup up to the boil and taste for salt.

Presentation:

Preheat an oven to 250°F/120°C. Warm the soup bowls in the oven. Ladle soup into each of the bowls. Garnish each bowl with a sprig of cilantro. Serve at once.

Oyster Stew

FOR THE SOUP BASE:

4$^1/_4$ cups/1 litre Chicken Stock (page 14)

3 Tbsp./45 mL butter

2 shallots, peeled and cut into brunoise

1 peeled potato, cut into small dice

FOR THE OYSTERS:

1 shallot, peeled and cut into brunoise

2 Tbsp./30 mL dry white wine

18 shucked Malpèque oysters

TO FINISH THE STEW:

1 egg yolk

2 Tbsp./30 mL 35% whipping cream

1 Tbsp./15 mL fino sherry

2 Tbsp./30 mL finely sliced chives

Freshly ground black pepper

Freshly grated nutmeg

▶Serves six

Heat the chicken stock in a saucepan until it is reduced by half its volume.

Preheat an oven to 350°F/175°C. Distribute the butter, shallots, and potato dice over a baking sheet. Cover with aluminum foil and place in the oven. The steam generated by the butter and shallots will cook the potato, so make sure the foil forms a good seal around the tray. Remove the tray from the oven when the potatoes are tender. Reserve.

Combine the shallots and wine in a small saucepan. Shuck the oysters into the saucepan and include the water from the shells. Discard the shells. When all the oysters are in the pot, simmer to gently poach them. The oysters should be barely cooked after about 1 minute once the liquid has reached simmering point.

Put three oysters and an equal amount of cooked potato dice into each bowl. Reduce the oven temperature to warm. Place the bowls in the oven. Bring the poaching liquid with the reduced chicken stock to the boil. Taste for salt. Add the sherry. Transfer the boiling liquid to a blender and blend. While the liquid is blending, drop in an egg yolk and add the whipping cream.

Presentation:

Remove the bowls from the oven. Pour some of the blended liquid into each bowl over the oysters. Garnish with chives, a twist of the peppermill, and a grating of fresh nutmeg. Serve at once.

Celery Root Soup with Blue Cheese Toasts

The combination of celery and blue cheese is a familiar one. Who hasn't tried Buffalo chicken wings with blue cheese dip and a side of celery sticks? This soup is a silky smooth, soul-warming presentation of a classic combination.

FOR THE SOUP:

1 Spanish onion, roughly chopped

1 potato, peeled and roughly chopped

2 Tbsp./30 mL butter

2 celery roots, peeled and roughly chopped

10 cups/2.5 litres Tomato Consommé (page 14)

FOR THE GARNISH:

2 slices of white bread, crusts removed

$^1/_4$ lb./113 g crumbled blue cheese

1 Tbsp./15 mL finely chopped chives

▶ Serves six

Gently sauté the onion and potato in the butter in a soup pot. After 5 minutes, add the celery root and the tomato consommé. Simmer for 40 minutes or until the celery root is very tender. Transfer the soup to a food processor and purée. Pass the soup through a sieve, return it to the pot, and keep at simmering point.

Preheat an oven to 275°F/135°C. Take the crusts off the bread and cut it into squares or triangles. Place the pieces on a baking sheet and toast them in the oven until they are golden.

Remove the tray from the oven. Carefully place crumbled blue cheese on each toasted triangle or square. Place the tray back in the oven until the cheese is melted.

Presentation:

Warm six soup bowls. Ladle soup into the bowls. Place one blue cheese croûton on each soup. Sprinkle with chopped chives and serve at once.

Seared Grouper
in Piquant Lemongrass Bouillon

FOR THE BOUILLON:

4¼ cups/1 litre Tomato Consommé (page 14)

1 trimmed stalk of lemongrass

2 green chilies, split lengthwise

FOR THE FISH:

2.2 lbs./1 kg grouper fillet

2 stalks of lemongrass

Salt to taste

2 Tbsp./30 mL sunflower oil

FOR THE GARNISH:

1 sweet potato, peeled and diced

1 leek, cleaned and diced

1 tomato, washed and diced

1 lemongrass stalk, trimmed and cut lengthwise into sixths

▶ Serves six

Bring the consommé to a simmer. Roughly chop the stalk of lemongrass and add to the consommé.

Add the chilies and continue to simmer and infuse for 30 minutes. Strain through a fine sieve. Discard the chilies and lemongrass. Reserve.

Cut the grouper across the grain into six equal pieces. Chop the tender inner leaves of the lemongrass finely. Place a sheet of plastic wrap or a plastic bag on the counter. Sprinkle with chopped lemongrass. Place two or three pieces of fish, depending on the size of the plastic, on the lemongrass. Sprinkle the fish with more lemongrass. Place a sheet of plastic on top of the fish. Pound with a meat pounder or the heel of a saucepan until the fillets are flattened to ⅜ inch/.95 cm thick. Repeat to flatten all of the fish.

Preheat an oven to 350°F/175°C. Place the sweet potatoes in an ovenproof frying pan in the oven. Bake, stirring from time to time, until tender but still firm. Add the leeks and continue to bake for 5 more minutes. Transfer the sweet potatoes and leeks to a stainless steel bowl. Mix in the tomato and reserve.

Use a large frying pan to heat the sunflower oil. Season the pieces of fish with salt. Fry the fish until golden on each side.

Presentation:

Warm six plates. Sprinkle the vegetable garnish on each plate and ladle some infused tomato consommé over it. Top the consommé with a piece of cooked fish. Garnish each plate with a lemongrass spear. Serve at once.

Warm Terrine of Salmon and Scallops

3 leeks, split and washed
3 lb./1.35 kg piece salmon fillet
Salt and freshly ground black pepper
1 lb./455 g sea scallops

1 clove garlic, finely chopped
1 Tbsp./15 mL pastis (see page 28)
Salt and freshly ground black pepper to taste

▶Serves six

Put a large soup pot of water on to boil. Blanch the leeks, leaf by leaf, in the water for 60 seconds. Carefully line the terrine form with the blanched leeks, leaving an overhang of 2 inches/5 cm on each side. Cut the salmon into pieces that fit the interior of the terrine. Cover the entire bottom of the terrine with one layer of salmon. Season liberally with salt and pepper.

Purée ¼ lb./113 g of the scallops in a food processor. Season the purée with salt and pepper, garlic, and pastis. Fold the remaining whole scallops into the purée. This mixture is the next layer in the terrine. Put a final layer of salmon fillet on top of the scallop mixture. Season liberally with salt and pepper. Fold the overhanging pieces of leek over the salmon. Put the lid on the terrine.

Preheat an oven to 350°F/175°C. Find a roasting pan that is longer than the terrine form. Line it with a tea towel and place the terrine form on the towel. Fill two-thirds of the roasting pan with hot water. Place the roasting pan with the terrine form in the oven. After 40 minutes, check the interior temperature of the terrine with a meat thermometer. The terrine is ready when the interior temperature reaches 150°F/65°C.

Invert the terrine onto a cutting board. You can serve it warm, straight out of the oven, or you can chill it and serve it cold with mayonnaise and a salad. If you decide to serve it warm, the best accompaniments are fresh steamed potatoes and vegetables. In either case, use a sharp carving knife to cut the terrine into ½-inch/1.2-cm slices.

To make this recipe you will need an enamelled cast iron terrine or pâté form with a lid. The standard one is approximately 10 inches/25 cm long and 3 inches/7.5 cm wide. As with so many great dishes, the most intense work is in the preparation. The service of this recipe is as easy as slicing bread. Dishes like this are good for dinner parties because you can be with your guests and still serve an interesting dinner.

Roasted Striped Bass in Olive Broth

This recipe reflects a Mediterranean influence. Garlic, olives, olive oil, and lemon are the cornerstones of this region's cooking tradition.

FOR THE BROTH:

1 cup/240 mL pitted Niçoise or Gaeta olives

2 cups/475 mL Tomato Consommé (page 14)

1 clove garlic, finely chopped

FOR THE GARNISH:

3 Tbsp./45 mL olive oil for cooking

6 cooked new potatoes, peeled and halved

1 clove garlic, finely chopped

1 Tbsp./15 mL fresh lemon juice

1 tsp./5 mL coarsely chopped fresh rosemary

1 bunch rapini, cleaned and trimmed

Salt and black pepper to taste

FOR THE FISH:

6, 5-oz./140-g fillets fresh striped bass

Salt and black pepper to taste

4 Tbsp./60 mL olive oil for cooking

$1/4$ cup/60 mL Roasted Red Pepper strips (page 155)

▶ Serves six

Put the olives in a food processor and purée. Warm the consommé to the simmering point and add the garlic. Keep the consommé simmering.

Heat the cooking oil in a large frying pan. Add the potatoes. When they are golden, add the garlic, lemon juice, and rosemary. Add the rapini and sauté for 3 minutes. Season with salt and pepper. Reserve.

Preheat an oven to 350°F/175°C. Season the fish liberally with salt and pepper. Fry skin side first in hot oil in an ovenproof frying pan. Turn the fillets over and finish cooking in the oven for 5 minutes. The fish is ready when the flesh is opaque and comes apart easily without being mushy.

Presentation:

Warm six plates. Place a mound of the potato rapini mixture in the center of each plate. Place a fish fillet on top of the potatoes. Transfer the olive purée to a blender. With the blender running, slowly pour in the simmering consommé. Pour some broth onto each plate. Garnish with the red pepper strips. Serve at once.

Facing page: Various preserves (pages 66, 111–15, 155–57)

Following page: Seared Grouper in Piquant Lemongrass Bouillon (page 174)

Poached Black Cod with Winter Vegetables
and Horseradish Sauce

FOR THE SAUCE:

1 Tbsp./15 mL butter

1 Tbsp./15 mL all purpose flour

1¹/₂ cups/360 mL milk

1 bay leaf

1 small onion, peeled

2 cloves

Salt to taste

3 Tbsp./45 mL peeled and freshly grated horseradish

FOR THE VEGETABLES:

6 small carrots, peeled and cooked

12 small potatoes, peeled and cooked

2 leeks, washed and cut into 2-inch/5 cm lengths

6 small beets, cooked and peeled

1, 2-inch/5-cm piece fresh horseradish

6 small sprigs of parsley

FOR THE FISH:

2-lb./900-g piece smoked black cod

▶ Serves six

Melt the butter in a saucepan over medium heat. Add the flour and stir with a wooden spoon. Be careful not to let the butter brown. Add the milk slowly, stirring continuously to avoid lumps. Fasten the bay leaf to the onion by tacking through the bay leaf with the cloves. Add the onion to the sauce and reduce the sauce to a simmer. Cook for 60 minutes, stirring from time to time. Add the grated horseradish to the sauce, then purée in a blender. Pass through a fine sieve.

Place a pot of water on to boil. Cut the fish into six equal pieces. Add the fish to the water, reduce to a simmer, and poach for 8 minutes.

Presentation:

Warm six plates. Reheat the vegetables by steaming them briefly, and arrange an equal amount on each plate. Transfer one fillet of fish to each plate. Nap each fillet with some sauce and garnish with a sprig of parsley and a grating of fresh horseradish. Serve at once.

One day a man brought me a sample of black cod from the West Coast to try. It didn't look like any cod I had ever seen because it wasn't really cod at all. Sometimes the real name of a product isn't judged marketable. Another example of this is sea bass, which really isn't a bass at all. Its real name is Patagonian Toothfish. I wonder if this species wouldn't today be on the verge of commercial extinction if it had been marketed by its real name. Those of you living on the West Coast should have no difficulty finding smoked black cod. If you can't find smoked cod, smoked mackerel could be substituted.

Facing page: Warm Chocolate Cake with Summer Fruits in Rum (page 191)

Previous page: Baked Meatloaf with Parsley (page 181)

Skate and Salmon Paupiettes
in Lemon and Parsley Sauce

FOR THE SALMON MOUSSE:

$^1/_2$-lb./227-g fresh salmon fillet

2 ice cubes

1 egg yolk

1 tsp./5 mL pastis (see page 28)

1 Tbsp./15 mL butter, softened to room temperature

2 Tbsp./30 mL 35% whipping cream

Salt to taste

FOR THE FISH:

2 lbs./900 g fresh skate wings (see page 134)

FOR THE SAUCE:

1 cup/240 mL dry Riesling or Sauvignon Blanc wine

1 Tbsp./15 mL peeled shallot, cut into brunoise

1 Tbsp./15 mL fresh lemon juice

2 Tbsp./30 mL chopped parsley

3 Tbsp./45 mL cold butter, cubed

FOR THE VEGETABLES:

12 small potatoes, cooked and peeled

▶ Serves six

Cut the salmon fillet into bite-sized pieces. Purée the pieces in a food processor with the ice cubes. While the motor is running, add the egg yolk and the pastis. Add the butter slowly. Then add the cream in a slow, steady stream. Season with salt. Reserve.

Lay out the skate wings with the flesh side down. Place some salmon mousse at one end of each fillet. Roll the fillet up so that the mousse is contained inside it. Wrap this paupiette with plastic film and twist the ends of the film to help keep a cylindrical shape. Repeat until all the paupiettes are rolled and wrapped. Steam the paupiettes in a vegetable steamer, covered, for 10 minutes. They are ready when the interior temperature reaches 150°F/165°C. Reserve.

Pour the wine into a saucepan over medium heat. Add the shallot brunoise. Boil down to a syrupy consistency. Add the lemon juice and boil for 30 seconds. Add the parsley and whisk in the butter.

Presentation:

Warm six plates. Remove the plastic film from the cooked paupiettes. Slice the paupiettes carefully with a sharp carving knife.

Arrange three slices in an overlapping pattern on each plate and nap with the sauce. Place two potatoes on each plate. Serve at once.

Cornish Hen Mirepoix

FOR THE CORNISH HEN:

2 carrots, peeled and finely sliced

2 onions, peeled and finely sliced

1 celery root, peeled and finely sliced

3 cloves garlic, peeled and finely sliced

2 green chilies, finely sliced

6 Tbsp./90 mL white wine vinegar

6 Cornish hens, boned

2 cups/480 mL sunflower oil

FOR THE SAUCE:

1 cup/240 mL Cornish Hen Jus (page 15) (substitute hen bones for chicken

FOR THE MASHED POTATOES:

1 recipe Mashed Potatoes (page 144)

2 Tbsp./30 mL coarsely chopped parsley

Salt to taste

▶Serves six

Prepare the marinade by mixing together the first six ingredients. Pour a layer of the marinade into the bottom of a baking dish. Place the hens in the marinade so that they are all covered. Place a weight on top (a can on top of a plate will do) to press down slightly.

Place the whole issue in the refrigerator for two days. Prepare the jus on the same day as you marinate the Cornish hens.

On the day that you are preparing the dish, separate the vegetables from the hens. Squeeze out the liquid from the mirepoix vegetables.

Heat the oil in a saucepan to 350°F/175°C. Fry the mirepoix until it's crisp and golden. Drain on paper towels. Lightly season with salt.

Prepare the mashed potatoes and keep them warm. Prepare a gas or charcoal barbeque. Season the Cornish hens liberally with salt and grill them until they are golden brown on both sides. Warm the jus in a small saucepan.

Presentation:

Warm six plates. Place a dollop of mashed potatoes in the center of each plate. Place one Cornish hen skin side up on the mashed potatoes. Place a small mound of crispy mirepoix on each hen. Spoon some jus on each plate. Garnish each plate with a sprinkling of parsley and serve at once.

This dish was inspired by the street fare at village markets in Portugal. Chicken piri-piri is a dish that originated during the Moorish occupation of the Iberian peninsula, but today is woven inextricably into Portuguese traditional cooking. The local cooks take out the backs of the chickens, marinate them with a mixture of olive oil, garlic, and chili peppers and splay them on a charcoal grill to cook slowly. Then they are sold by the half with litre bottles of wine from the Alentejo. It is a crowded scene.

In this adaptation, more of the bones are removed. Because I use Cornish hens, the whole bird makes a single serving. The mirepoix adds aromatic flavors to the marinade and to the final presentation.

Filled Quail with Sage Risotto

Boning the quail is an arduous task. There isn't really a scientific way to approach it. It is rather primal and gory, so keep a stiff upper lip. The idea is to remove the bones from the cavity so that when they are all removed the quail's form is still recognizable.

Do not add salt to the cooking water for the beans. In some areas, depending on the minerals present in the water, salt may cause the beans to stay hard even with prolonged cooking. Discard cooking water before adding the cooked beans to the bread mixture.

FOR THE QUAIL:
6 quail, boned

FOR THE FILLING:
2 slices of white bread, crusts removed
2 Tbsp./30 mL milk
1/2 cup/120 mL cooked romano beans (see Note)
1 tsp./5 mL roughly chopped fresh sage
Salt and freshly ground black pepper to taste

1 Tbsp./15 mL olive oil for cooking
Salt and black pepper to taste

FOR THE RISOTTO:
1 Tbsp./15 mL olive oil for cooking
1 cup/240 mL short grain Italian rice
2 cloves garlic, split in half
2 cups/480 mL Chicken Stock (page 14)
2 Tbsp./60 mL white wine
2 Tbsp./30 mL 35% whipping cream
1/4 cup/60 mL grated Parmigiano Reggiano
1 Tbsp./15 mL roughly chopped fresh sage

▶ Serves six

Bone the quails.

Cut the bread into cubes. Soak the bread cubes in milk. Add the cooked beans to the soaked bread. Add the sage and season with salt and pepper. Fill the cavity of the boneless quails with this mixture.

Preheat an oven to 350°F/175°C. Heat the olive oil in a frying pan on medium heat. Season the quail with salt and pepper. Sear the quail on all sides. Roast the quail in the oven for 15 minutes or until the interior temperature reaches 150°F/65°C.

Pour the olive oil for the risotto into a large frying pan on medium heat. Warm the chicken stock in a saucepan. Add the rice and toast, stirring continuously, until it is golden brown. Add the garlic pieces. Add the chicken stock gradually, stirring continuously, until it is all absorbed by the rice. Add the white wine, cream, cheese, and sage. Mix thoroughly.

Presentation:

Warm six plates. Place a mound of risotto on each plate. Place a quail on each mound of risotto. Spoon any drippings from the quail pan onto each plate. Serve at once.

Baked Meatloaf with Parsley
and Fried Potatoes

FOR THE MEATLOAF:

3 slices white bread

4 Tbsp./60mL milk

1 Spanish onion, peeled and diced

2 Tbsp./30 mL butter

1 lb./455 g ground beef

1 lb./455 g ground pork

2 eggs

2 Tbsp./30 mL roughly chopped parsley

$1/4$ tsp./5 mL freshly grated nutmeg

Salt and freshly ground black pepper to taste

2 cups/480 mL Tomato Sauce (page 156)

FOR THE SAUCE:

1 cup/240 mL Beef Jus (page 15)

Salt and freshly ground black pepper to taste

FOR THE POTATOES:

12 small potatoes, cooked

3 Tbsp./45 mL unsalted butter

2 Tbsp./30 mL roughly chopped parsley

Salt to taste

This dish epitomizes the notion of comfort food. Even if your mother didn't prepare meatloaf for you as a child this recipe is sure to evoke some feeling of warmth.

▶Serves six

Remove the crusts from the bread and cut the bread into small cubes. Place the cubes in a stainless steel mixing bowl with the milk. Gently sauté the onion in the butter for 5 minutes. Transfer to the mixing bowl with the soaked bread. Add the rest of the meatloaf ingredients, except for the tomato sauce. Mix well and transfer mixture to a meatloaf pan or enamelled terrine form. Cook the tomato sauce in a saucepan over medium heat to reduce to a thick consistency.

Preheat an oven to 350°F/175°C. Spread the reduced tomato sauce on the meatloaf and bake for 40 minutes or until the interior temperature reaches 150°F/65°C.

Pour the beef jus into a saucepan to warm.

Peel the cooked potatoes and slice them into rounds. Sauté the potatoes in the butter until they are golden brown on both sides. Season with salt and sprinkle with parsley.

Presentation:

Warm six plates. Cut a thick slice of meatloaf and transfer to the center of each plate. Surround the slices with fried potatoes. Pour jus over the meatloaf. Serve at once.

Braised Brisket of Beef
with Beer and Onion Sauce

*U*se brisket points for this recipe. This is the cut preferred for corned beef and gives great results for this dish. This takes a bit of preparation to get started, but then you could go out tobogganing for a few hours and come back to the cozy house with warm smells wafting from the kitchen.

2 Spanish onions, peeled and sliced
3 Tbsp./45 mL unsalted butter
2 cups/480 mL beer
1 cup/240 mL Tomato Sauce (page 156)

1 bay leaf
1 Tbsp./15 mL sunflower oil
3-lb./1.35-kg piece beef brisket point
Salt to taste

▶ Serves six

Preheat an oven to 275°F/135°C. Gently sauté the onions in the butter for 20 minutes or until they are golden brown. Add the beer and the tomato sauce. Bring to a boil, add the bay leaf, and simmer.

Place a large frying pan on high heat. Add the sunflower oil. Place the brisket in the frying pan to sear. When it is brown on the bottom, turn it over. When it is brown on both sides, transfer it to an oven dish with a lid. Pour the simmering sauce over the brisket. Place the lid on top and braise in the oven for 3 hours.

Presentation:

Warm six plates. Carve slices of braised brisket onto each plate. Nap each plate with the beer and onion sauce. Serve with Mashed Potatoes (page 144) and a green salad.

Prime Rib of Beef with Two Sauces

FOR THE BEEF:

1, 5-lb./2.25-kg standing rib of beef

1 Tbsp./15 mL roughly chopped thyme

1 Tbsp./15 mL coarsely ground black pepper

2 cloves garlic, finely chopped

Salt to taste

2 Tbsp./30 mL sunflower oil

1 cup/240 mL Pinot Noir wine

FOR THE PARSLEY-HORSERADISH SAUCE:

1 cup/240 mL Béchamel sauce (page 177)

1 cup/240 mL Italian parsley leaves

$^1/_2$ cup/120 mL freshly grated horseradish root

The two sauces give the finished plates an interesting contrast of color and flavor. The deep red brown of the deglazed pan juices emphasizes the bright green of the parsley-horseradish sauce.

▶ Serves six

Preheat an oven to 350°F/175°C. Rub the beef with the thyme, pepper, and garlic. Sprinkle the beef liberally with salt. Place the rib in a roasting pan. Cover with the sunflower oil and place in the oven.

Roast for 90 minutes, basting periodically. Remove from the oven when desired doneness is achieved. Deglaze with the wine as for Roast Lamb (page 184) and reserve.

To make the parsley-horseradish sauce, first prepare the béchamel sauce. Boil water in a soup pot. Add the parsley leaves to the boiling water for 10 minutes. Strain the leaves and purée them in a blender. Add the puréed parsley and the grated horseradish to the béchamel sauce and pass the sauce through a fine strainer. Reserve.

Presentation:

Warm six plates. Carve a slice of roast onto each plate. Spoon a pool of the deglazed pan juices and a pool of the horseradish sauce on each plate with the beef. Grate fresh horseradish onto each plate. Mashed potatoes and roasted root vegetables make a great accompaniment to this dish.

Roast Leg of Lamb with Gratin Potatoes
and Green Beans

It used to be that the best lamb was available only in the spring, around Easter. Now, because so many more people enjoy lamb, you can purchase it all year round. For this recipe ask your local butcher for a 3-lb./ 1.35-kg leg.

FOR THE LAMB:

1, 3-lb./1.35-kg leg of lamb

2 cloves garlic, finely chopped

2 Tbsp./30 mL roughly chopped fresh rosemary

1 tsp./5 mL coarsely ground black peppercorns

Salt to taste

2 Tbsp./30 mL olive oil for cooking

1/2 cup/120 mL Cabernet Sauvignon wine

FOR THE GRATIN:

6 medium Yukon Gold potatoes

2 cloves garlic, finely chopped

1 tsp./5 mL roughly chopped fresh thyme

2 shallots, peeled and cut into brunoise

1 cup/240 mL 35% whipping cream

1 cup/240 mL Gruyère cheese, grated

Salt and freshly ground black pepper to taste

FOR THE GREEN BEANS:

1 lb./455 g trimmed green beans

2 Tbsp./30 mL unsalted butter

2 shallots, peeled and cut into brunoise

Salt and freshly ground black pepper to taste

▶Serves six

Preheat an oven to 350°F/175°C. Rub the lamb with garlic, rosemary, and pepper. Sprinkle liberally with salt.

Put the lamb in a roasting pan. Pour olive oil all over the leg of lamb and roast for 1 hour, basting periodically.

Check doneness with a meat thermometer inserted in the thickest part of the leg. 120°F/ 45°C = rare, 160°F/75°C = well done. Remove the roast from the oven when the desired doneness is achieved. (I prefer medium-rare, 140°F/55°C.) Discard most of the fat from the roasting pan, but keep the juices in the pan. Deglaze with the Cabernet Sauvignon and place the roasting pan directly over a medium burner to boil the wine with the juices until the volume has reduced by three-quarters. Reserve.

Peel the potatoes and slice them as thinly as possible. A mandolin is the best tool to use for this. Use a large stainless steel bowl to mix together all the ingredients for the gratin. Transfer the ingredients to a baking dish. The top layer should be neatly arranged in overlapping slices. Cover the dish with aluminum foil and place it in the oven for 45 minutes. Remove the foil and bake for an additional 20 minutes. The top should be golden brown. Remove from the oven.

Blanch the green beans for 5 minutes in rapidly boiling water. Drain and cool. Melt the butter in a saucepan.

Sauté the beans for 3 minutes in the butter over medium heat. Add the shallots and sauté for 5 more minutes. Season with salt and pepper.

Presentation:

Warm six plates. Cut a piece of gratin onto each plate. Place the beans in a random pattern on and beside the gratin. Carve three slices of lamb and place them beside the gratin. Spoon some deglazed pan juices over the lamb. Serve immediately.

Toasting Lance at JK ROM.

Roast and Braise of Venison
with Wild Rice Spaetzle

Spaetzle is a handmade noodle. It hails from several mountainous European countries. It's difficult to say where it originated from exactly, but the question is the source of heated debate among Germans, Swiss, and Austrians. I have given my spaetzle recipe a distinctly Canadian accent, with the addition of some ground wild rice.

As with all stews, the venison braise will improve overnight. As Huckleberry Finn observes in Mark Twain's famous novel, "it gives a chance for the flavors to swap around."

FOR THE VENISON:

3 lbs./1.35 kg fresh venison leg

1, 25-oz./750-mL bottle Cabernet Sauvignon wine

6 crushed juniper berries

12 cracked black peppercorns

2 bay leaves

2 Spanish onions

1 celery root, scrubbed

1 carrot, scrubbed

1 washed leek

1 sprig fresh thyme

2 Tbsp./30 mL sunflower oil

FOR THE SPAETZLE:

7 eggs

1 1/2 cups/360 mL all purpose flour

1/2 cup/120 mL ground wild rice

1/4 tsp./5 mL freshly grated nutmeg

Salt to taste

2 Tbsp./30 mL unsalted butter

▶ Serves six

Ask the butcher to separate the muscles in the leg of venison for you. Divide the meat roughly in half. The parts that are closer to the shank will be less tender. Use these parts for the braise. Cut the braising pieces into large cubes, and leave the roasting pieces whole. Cut the vegetables into fairly large, equal pieces. Set the braising meat in a marinade made up of half the wine and half the vegetables, and herbs. Set the roasting pieces in a marinade made up of the remaining wine, vegetables, and herbs. Place the marinating meats in the refrigerator for one week.

The day before you plan to serve this dish, prepare the braise and the spaetzle.

Preheat an oven to 375°F/190°C. Strain the wine and the vegetables from the braising meat.

Place the vegetables on a baking sheet and place it in the oven to roast. Simmer the marinating liquid in a saucepan. When it reaches simmering point, the proteins in the liquid will coagulate. When this has occurred, strain the liquid through a cheesecloth. The clear liquid that remains will be the braising medium.

Sear the meat in a hot frying pan with the sunflower oil. Transfer the meat to a braising or stewing pot with a lid.

When the vegetables roasting in the oven have browned nicely, add them to the meat. Add the braising liquid and season with salt. Cover the pot and place it in the oven. Check for doneness after 45 minutes. The meat should be tender, but not falling apart.

In a stainless steel bowl, mix together all the

ingredients for the spaetzle. Beat the mixture vigorously for 5 minutes to release gluten to strengthen the dough. Set a soup pot full of salted water on to boil. The true artisanal method of making spaetzle, taught to me by my friend and colleague, Michael Stadtländer, is to use a small wooden board and a spatula to drop strands of dough into the boiling water. Most of us need to use a spaetzle extruder, which can be found in most kitchen specialty shops. In any case, you boil the spaetzle noodles for 3 minutes, cool them in ice water, then drain them on tea towels before frying them in butter. Keep the braise and the spaetzle in the refrigerator overnight.

Preheat an oven to 375°F/190°C. Separate the roasting pieces from the vegetables and herbs. Set the vegetables and herbs on a baking sheet and place them in the oven. Bring the marinating liquid to the simmering point in a saucepan. Strain and add this liquid to the braise. Add the roasted vegetables to the braise as well. Bring the braise to the simmering point and hold there. Season the roasting pieces with salt. Sear them in a large frying pan set on high heat. Transfer them to the oven to roast. Check for doneness after 10 minutes by inserting a meat thermometer into the thickest piece (page 184). I prefer to serve venison rare at 120°F/45°C. Remove to a carving board to relax 10 minutes before carving.

Melt the butter for the spaetzle in a large frying pan. When it is sizzling add the spaetzle. Season with salt. Sauté spaetzle until it is golden brown on all sides.

Presentation:
Warm six plates. Place some braised venison with the vegetables and juice on each plate, surrounded by spaetzle. Add three slices of roasted venison. Serve at once.

Eggplant Gâteau with Creamy Polenta

This is a great vegetarian dish that can be prepared quickly in the winter using foods that you have preserved in the summer or fall. Of course, if you haven't done any preserving, these vegetables are still available fresh in the winter. The problem is that they are super-expensive and taste like cardboard.

1 quart/1 litre jar Marinated Eggplant (page 157)
1 quart/1 litre jar Roasted Red Peppers (page 155)
1 lb./455 g bocconcini or pressed ricotta
1/2 cup/120 mL corn meal
1 1/2 cups/360 mL water

Salt to taste
2 Tbsp./30 mL 35% whipping cream
2 Tbsp./30 mL grated Parmigiano Reggiano
1 quart/1 litre jar Tomato Sauce (page 156)

▶Serves six

Preheat an oven to 350°F/175°C. Use individual baking dishes to make this dish. Layer alternating slices of eggplant, peppers, and bocconcini in each dish. There should be six slices in each dish. Make sure the top slice is bocconcini. Place the baking dishes in the oven.

Meanwhile, simmer the tomato sauce on the stove in a saucepan. Prepare the creamy polenta in another saucepan by boiling the water and adding the corn meal. Stir for 3 minutes. Add the cream and grated cheese.

Presentation:

Remove the baking dishes from the oven when they are bubbling and the cheese has melted. Pour some creamy polenta into the base of each dish. Spoon some tomato sauce over each dish. Serve at once.

Baked Apple and Chestnut Tart

FOR THE PASTRY:
1 lb./455 g Sweet Pastry (page 24)

FOR THE FILLING:
1 cup/240 mL Chestnut Purée (page 154)
8 apples, peeled, cored and sliced
1/2 tsp./2.5 mL freshly grated nutmeg
1/2 tsp./2.5 mL freshly grated cinnamon
4 Tbsp. /60 mL sugar plus 1/2 cup/120 mL

4 eggs
1/2 cup/120 mL sifted pastry flour
1/3 cup/90 mL melted butter

FOR THE GLAZE:
2 cups/480 mL natural apple cider

FOR THE GARNISH:
1 cup/240 mL whipped 35% whipping cream

Use a deep, scalloped 10-inch/25-cm tart form with a removable base. These forms are common in French pastry-making and may be found in kitchen specialty shops.

▶ Serves six

Preheat an oven to 350°F/175°C. Grease and flour the tart form. After chilling the sweet pastry for at least 2 hours, roll it out to a thickness of 1/3 inch/.85 cm. Roll the pastry up on the rolling pin and unroll it gradually, draping it loosely over the surface of the tart form.

Press the pastry into every nook and cranny of the form. Fill the form with baking beans and blind bake in the oven for 30 minutes or until the pastry is golden brown.

Prepare the chestnut purée and reserve it at room temperature. Mix the apples, nutmeg, cinnamon, and 4 Tbsp./60 mL sugar in a stainless steel bowl. In another stainless steel bowl combine the eggs and 1/2 cup/120 mL sugar. Whisk in the bowl over a simmering pot of water until the egg mixture is slightly warmer than body temperature. Remove from the heat and continue to whisk vigorously to lighten the mixture and increase its volume. Whisk until it resembles thick mayonnaise. Fold in the flour and the melted butter.

Spread the chestnut purée over the base of the prebaked tart form. Drain the excess liquid from the apples and fold them into the egg mixture. Spread this mixture on top of the chestnut purée. Bake for 30 minutes or until the apples are soft and the mixture is set.

Boil the apple cider in a stainless steel pot over high heat. Reduce to a syrupy consistency. Paint over the surface of the baked tart.

Presentation:

Put a wedge of apple tart on each plate. Serve warm or at room temperature with a dollop of whipped cream.

Grapefruit and Champagne Granité

If you do not have an ice cream machine, then making granité is the next best thing. Actually, granité is more popular in Italian culture where it is called granita. There, you will see vendors selling it from kiosks as a refreshment not so far removed from our own beloved snow cones. Here, I offer it as a refreshing light dessert or as a delightful pause between the fish and meat courses in a gastronomic menu.

FOR THE GRANITÉ:

3 cups/360 mL fresh grapefruit juice

3/4 cup/180 mL sugar

1/2 cup/120 mL Champagne or other sparkling white wine

▶Serves six

Mix the grapefruit juice with the sugar until it dissolves. Add the champagne. Pour the mixture into a glass oven dish and place the dish in the freezer. Stir the freezing granité from time to time. After 1 hour, ice crystals should begin to form. Keep stirring until the mixture resembles a grainy, thick slush.

FOR THE GARNISH:

12 grapefruit sections

6 small sprigs of mint

1/2 cup/120 mL Champagne or other sparkling white wine

Presentation:

Chill six Champagne saucers or martini glasses. Spoon some granité into each glass. Add two sections of grapefruit and one small mint sprig to each glass. Just before serving, pour some Champagne into each glass.

Warm Chocolate Cake
with Summer Fruits in Rum

FOR THE CAKE:

1¼ cups/300 mL grated semisweet chocolate

4 Tbsp./60 mL butter

5 egg yolks

¼ cup/60 mL sugar

2 egg whites

Pinch of salt

FOR THE ICE CREAM:

3 cups/720 mL Crème Anglaise (page 19)

FOR THE SUMMER FRUITS IN RUM:

1½ cups/360 mL Summer Fruits in Rum
(page 111)

This recipe is another example of taking preserved foods from one season and combining them with something fresh for a new and delicious result. This is a flourless chocolate cake served warm. The best forms to use for the cake batter are individual brioche forms with deep scalloped sides. These are available at kitchen supply stores.

▶ Serves six

Melt the chocolate and butter in a stainless steel bowl over a simmering pan of water and reserve. Place the egg yolks and half the sugar in another stainless steel bowl. Whisk until the mixture lightens in texture and color and forms a ribbon as it falls back upon itself. Fold the egg yolk mixture into the chocolate butter mixture. Whip the egg whites with the remaining sugar. Fold the egg whites into the chocolate mixture.

If you are making the ice cream yourself, put the crème anglaise into the ice cream maker and process.

Preheat an oven to 350°F/175°C. Grease the cake forms with butter and dust with flour. Pour the batter into the forms so they are two-thirds full. Bake for 10 minutes or until the batter is just set. The center of the cake should still be almost molten.

Presentation:

Place some summer fruits in rum on six plates. Unmold the chocolate cakes while they are still warm, right onto the fruits. Spoon a scoop of ice cream onto the cake. Serve at once.

Orange Salad with Cocoa Sorbet

Citrus fruits are at their best during the winter months. In some areas, unusual varieties of oranges are available. This recipe works well with regular navel oranges, but if you come across blood oranges, try them instead. Their unique coloring and tartness offer a good contrast to the sweet richness of the cocoa sorbet.

FOR THE SORBET:

8 Tbsp./120 mL sugar

¹/₂ vanilla pod

3 cups/720 mL water

8 Tbsp./120 mL cocoa powder

FOR THE SALAD:

6 navel or blood oranges

2 Tbsp./30 mL sugar

FOR THE GARNISH:

6 mint leaves, cut into fine julienne

▶ Serves six

Place the sugar in a saucepan. Split the vanilla pod in half lengthwise. Scrape out the resinous gum and add it and the husk to the pot with the sugar. Add the water and simmer until all the sugar is dissolved. Place the cocoa powder in a stainless steel bowl. Add the vanilla syrup a little at a time, while whisking, until it is a paste consistency. This method prevents lumps from forming. Add the rest of the syrup and transfer to an ice cream maker. Process.

Use a paring knife to remove the skin and membrane surrounding the orange segments. Using the natural division of the segments as your guide, cut out orange sections that have no pith or membrane attached to them. Squeeze the juice from the orange membranes into a small saucepan. Boil the juice and sugar until the mixture has a syrupy consistency.

Presentation:

Chill six plates and lay them out on the counter. Arrange the orange sections in a circular pattern on the plates. Drizzle the sections with orange syrup. Leave a circle in the middle wide enough to hold a scoop of cocoa sorbet. Carefully scoop the sorbet into the center of each plate. Sprinkle each plate with the fine julienne of mint. Serve at once.

Nutmeg Ice Cream in Poppy Seed Crepe
with Sour Cherry Glaze

FOR THE ICE CREAM:

1 recipe Crème Anglaise (page 19)

$^1/_2$ tsp./2.5 mL freshly grated nutmeg

FOR THE CREPES:

1 recipe Crepe Batter (page 20)

1 cup/240 mL ground poppy seeds

FOR THE SOUR CHERRY GLAZE:

1 recipe Sour Cherry Consommé (page 89)

2 Tbsp./30 mL sugar

Icing sugar for dusting

▶ Serves six

Mix the crème anglaise with the grated nutmeg. Transfer to an ice cream maker and process.

After preparing the crepe batter, add the ground poppy seeds and allow the batter to rest for 1 hour. Use a large nonstick frying pan to make crepes. Finished crepes should measure approximately 8 inches/20 cm across. Prepare six crepes.

Pour the sour cherry consommé into a stainless steel saucepan. Add the sugar.

Simmer until the liquid has reached a syrupy stage. Reserve.

Presentation:

Chill six soup bowls. Lay the crepes out on the counter. Place a large scoop of ice cream in the center of each crepe.

Fold the crepe over and place it in the center of each bowl. Spoon some of the sour cherry glaze into each bowl. Dust with icing sugar. Serve at once.

Brandy Snap with Gingerbread Mousse
and Preserved Plums

You only need six brandy snaps for this recipe so there will be a lot of leftover dough for using another time or for making a batch of cookies now. The same applies to the gingerbread. Both may be frozen for future use.

FOR THE BRANDY SNAPS:

¹/₂ cup/120 mL brown sugar

¹/₂ cup/120 mL butter

¹/₂ cup/120 mL corn syrup

³/₄ cup/180 mL sifted pastry flour

¹/₃ cup/75 mL crushed walnuts

1 tsp./5 mL brandy

1 Tbsp./15 mL chopped fresh ginger

1 Tbsp./15 mL molasses

FOR THE GINGERBREAD:

10¹/₂ cups/2.5 litres sifted all purpose flour

3 Tbsp./45 mL baking powder

2 tsp./10 mL salt

4 tsp./20 mL ground cinnamon

2 tsp./10 mL ground cloves

2 tsp./10 mL ground black pepper

2 Tbsp./30 mL chopped fresh ginger

1 lb./455 g butter

2¹/₂ cups/600 mL brown sugar

8 eggs

2 cups/480 mL molasses

3 cups/720 mL fresh coffee

2 Tbsp./30 mL rum

FOR THE MOUSSE:

5 tbsp./75 mL sugar

1 Tbsp./15 mL rum

3 egg yolks

1¹/₂ cups/360 mL coarsely crumbled gingerbread

2 gelatin leaves, soaked in cold water

2 cups/480 mL 35% whipping cream

FOR THE POACHED PLUMS:

1 quart/1 litre jar Plums in Vanilla Syrup (page 111)

▶Serves six

To make the brandy snap dough, bring the sugar, butter, and syrup to a boil. Combine with the other ingredients in a stainless steel bowl. Mix well and chill for 2 hours in the refrigerator.

Preheat an oven to 375°F/175°C for the gingerbread. In a mixing bowl sift together the flour, baking powder, salt, and dry spices. Add the chopped fresh ginger. In another bowl cream the butter and sugar together. Beat in the eggs one at a time. Mix in the molasses. Add the flour mixture and the coffee alternately to the egg mixture until both are incorporated. Pour into a baking sheet lined with greased parchment paper and bake for 30 minutes or until the top of the cake springs back when touched. Cool and crumble into large pieces.

For the mousse, combine the sugar, rum, and egg yolks in a stainless steel bowl. Suspend over a simmering pot of water, whisking continuously to make a sabayon. Take care not to curdle the egg yolks here. It works well if you lift the sabayon bowl from the heat source from time to time. As the sabayon becomes lighter in texture there is less likelihood that it will curdle. Squeeze the excess water from the soaking gelatin and add the gelatin to the sabayon. Sprinkle the rum over the gingerbread. Fold the gingerbread into the sabayon. Whip the cream to stiff peaks. Fold the cream into the sabayon. Chill.

Lower the oven temperature to 325°F/165°C. Take the brandy snap dough from the refrigerator and roll it into balls 1 inch/2.5 cm wide. Place the balls on a greased cookie sheet. Wet your finger to flatten the dough slightly. Bake for 15 minutes or until the snaps spread out and have a lacy appearance.

Take them out of the oven and cool them slightly before draping them over a broom handle, laid horizontally between two chairbacks, to cool thoroughly. Draping them over a broom handle in this manner gives them a summit roof tile or tuile shape.

Presentation:

Lay out six plates. Hold a brandy snap in one hand and carefully scoop some mousse into the curve of the brandy snap. Repeat until all the brandy snaps are filled. Place a filled brandy snap on each plate, with two poached plums on either side. Drizzle some of the juice from the jar over each plum. Serve at once.

Old Cheddar Crisp
with Blackberry Poached Pear

This is a great dish to have if you are drinking red wine with dinner and still have some wine in the glass after the main course is finished. The Cheddar and the blackberry flavors pick up complementary notes in the wine.

FOR THE PEARS:

2 cups/480 mL Blackberry Purée (page 114)

3 ripe, firm pears

1 cup/240 mL water

FOR THE CRISPS:

6 slices whole wheat bread

1 lb./455 g old Cheddar cheese

2 cups/480 mL mixed salad greens

2 Tbsp./30 mL fine olive oil

Salt and freshly ground black pepper to taste

▶Serves six

Pour the blackberry purée into a stainless steel saucepan. Add the water and bring to the simmering point. Peel the pears carefully with a paring knife, conforming to the natural curves and undulations of the pear. Take out the core with a melon baller. Place the peeled pears in the blackberry poaching liquid. Cover and simmer for 30 minutes, turning pears occasionally during the cooking. Let the pears cool in the poaching liquid so they have a chance to absorb as much color and flavor from the blackberry as possible.

Preheat an oven to 250°F/120°C. Take the crusts off the bread and cut the slices in half to form triangles. Open the oven door and drape the slices of bread over the oven racks so that, as they toast, they will dry and set in a curved shape.

Cut the Cheddar into six wedges. Allow the cheese to come to room temperature.

Dress the salad with olive oil and seasonings.

Presentation:

Pool some blackberry purée in the center of each plate. Place a small mound of salad in the center of each pool of purée. Place two crisps cradling the wedge of Cheddar on the salad. Cut the pears in sixths lengthwise and place two pieces in each of the crisps with the cheese. Serve at once.

Cream Puff with Vanilla Mousse
and Chocolate Sauce

FOR THE CREAM PUFFS:

1 recipe Choux Pastry (page 22)

FOR THE VANILLA MOUSSE:

1 vanilla bean

3 egg yolks

6 Tbsp./90 mL sugar

2 gelatin leaves soaked in cold water

1 1/2 cups/360 mL 35% whipping cream

FOR THE CHOCOLATE SAUCE:

6 Tbsp./90 mL grated semisweet chocolate

6 tsp./30 mL homogenized milk

▶ Serves six

Preheat an oven to 350°F/175°C. Place a large star tip in a large piping bag. Fill the bag with the choux pastry. Line a baking sheet with silicone paper. Pipe 18 rosettes measuring 1 inch/2.5 cm wide by 1 inch/2.5 cm high onto the baking sheet. Bake until golden brown. Remove the tray from the oven to cool.

Split the vanilla bean in half and scrape out the resinous gum. Mix the egg yolks in a stainless steel bowl with the vanilla and add the sugar.

Whisk continuously in the same bowl over a simmering pan of water until the sabayon has lightened in texture and color. Squeeze the excess water from the gelatin leaves and add the gelatin to the warm sabayon. Mix well to melt the gelatin.

Whip the cream to stiff peaks and fold it into the vanilla sabayon. Transfer the mousse to a piping bag fitted with a large plain tip. Poke a hole in the bottom of each cream puff. Using the piping bag, fill the cream puffs with vanilla mousse.

Place the grated chocolate in a stainless steel bowl. Melt the chocolate over a pan of simmering water. When the chocolate has melted, add the milk and stir to a sauce consistency.

Presentation:

Place three filled cream puffs on each of six plates. Drizzle chocolate liberally over the cream puffs. Serve at once.

Glossary

Bain-marie: A hot water bath used as a source of indirect heat for cooking (see *Sabayon*) or keeping food warm (a double boiler is a kind of bain-marie).

Batons: Sticks of vegetables approximately 1½ inches/4 cm long and ¼ inch/6 mm thick.

Blanch: Literally, to whiten; a preliminary process in which foods are immersed briefly in boiling water (often just until the water returns to the boil); they are usually then refreshed in cold water.

Blind bake: To bake an empty pie or tart shell. Small weights, or baking beans, are used to weigh the pastry down so that it doesn't expand or bubble during baking.

Brunoise: A mixture of vegetables cut in uniform ⅛-inch/3-mm dice.

Chiffonade: A garnish of lettuce or other leafy vegetables cut in julienne.

Clarification: The process of removing impurities from liquids; in the case of consommés, egg whites and flavoring ingredients are boiled up with the liquid to form a raft.

Clarified butter: To make, simmer the butter gently until all the liquid separates from the melted butter by evaporation. Skim from time to time. Strain through a fine sieve.

Concassé (concasser): Literally, to break up; the term is usually applied to tomatoes that have been peeled and seeded and are then roughly chopped—I generally cut them in ½-inch/12-mm squares.

Confit: Derived from the French confir (to preserve), this is a traditional preparation for preserving food. Confit of duck leg is mildly brined and cooked very slowly in duck fat. The fat seals the duck, which may be preserved for months without refrigeration.

Court bouillon: "Bouillon" means something that is cooked for a long time, whereas its opposite, court bouillon, means a quick, short (5 to 10 minute) boil. Usually a court bouillon requires boiling aromatic vegetables with savoury flavoring to be used as a poaching liquid.

Deglaze: To clean out the pan used for roasting or frying by adding liquid (usually wine) and scraping up the brown bits from the bottom; the resulting mixture is the foundation of the sauce of the dish to be prepared.

Floret: The heads of cauliflower and broccoli can be broken into smaller, flower-shaped pieces called florets.

Fumet: Fish stock, best made from flat salt-water species such as flounder, plaice, or sole (freshwater fish are too oily).

Gratiné (gratiner): To brown with top heat in an oven or under a broiler.

Julienne: Fine sticks—usually vegetables—about $\frac{1}{8}$-inch/3-mm wide and 2 inches/5 cm long.

Lardons: Sticks of bacon approximately $1\frac{1}{2}$ inches/4 cm long and $\frac{1}{4}$ inch/6 mm thick.

Mirepoix: A mixture of onion, carrot, and celery cut in uniform $\frac{3}{4}$-inch/2-cm cubes; used for flavoring basic stocks and sauces.

Olive oil, fine: Olive oil that is much more fruity and aromatic than cooking-quality olive oil. This finer oil, called extra virgin olive oil, is extracted from the olives without heat and should not be used for cooking because it will lose some of its flavor and aroma. Fine olive oil is better used as a condiment or salad dressing.

Olive oil for cooking: Lesser quality olive oil that has been subjected to heat to extract it from the olives; perfectly suited to cooking. Because it has already been heated, there is no risk that it will lose any of its delicate aroma.

Raft: The mass that floats to the surface of a bouillon during the process of clarification and collects impurities as the liquid percolates through it.

Reduce: To boil a liquid until most of the moisture evaporates, in order to concentrate the flavor.

Rosettes: Piped shapes resembling roses.

Sabayon: A mixture of egg yolks and flavorings (sweet or savory) beaten over indirect heat to produce a heavy froth with the consistency of a thick mayonnaise.

Sauté (sauter): Literally, to jump; to fry quickly, tossing and stirring, in a small amount of oil or butter.

Zest: The thinly peeled or grated colored outer skin (without any white) of citrus fruit.

Index

Entries in italic are featured in the recipe introductions.